London Lines

THE PLACES AND FACES OF LONDON
IN POETRY AND SONG

an anthology selected by
KENNETH BAKER

with photographs by David Lister

METHUEN

by the same author

I Have No Gun But I Can Spit

First published in 1982 by Methuen London Ltd
11 New Fetter Lane, London EC4P 4EE

This anthology © 1982 by Kenneth Baker

Individual poems ©
as indicated in Acknowledgements

British Library Cataloguing in Publication Data

London lines.
　1. English poetry　　2. London (England)—
Literary collections
I. Baker, Kenneth
821'.008'032421　　PR1195.L6

ISBN 0-413-49460-8

Printed in Great Britain
by Butler & Tanner Ltd, Frome and London
The lines quoted on the back of the jacket are taken from A. S. J. Tessimond's
poem London, *which is quoted in full on page 19*

LONDON LINES

FOR MARY

CONTENTS

In the notes at the end of the book some information is given about some anonymous or less well-known poets whose work is included.

The places and people photographed in the illustrations, and the pages on which they appear, are as follows:

Central London from Parliament Hill (page 2); Middle Temple (12); The Statue of Eros, Piccadilly Circus (17); St James's Park (18); A porter at Smithfield Market (25); St Paul's from the South-East (26); Smithfield Market (36); The Post Office Tower from the junction of Euston Road and Hampstead Road (39); Kite-flying, Parliament Hill (40); A political demonstration, Trafalgar Square (53); Dr Johnson's Statue, Clement Dane's Church, Fleet Street (54); Ruby Braff at the *Pizza Express*, Wardour Street (69); The Mall (70); York Bridge, the approach to Queen Mary's Gardens, Regent's Park (79); The Thames from Waterloo Bridge, with barges (80); Portobello Road market (84); St James's Park (85); Kilburn Park Underground Station (88); Buskers at Charing Cross (95); A bus in Oxford Street (96); Liverpool Street Station (97); The Dean's Cloister, Westminster Abbey (101); The entrance to The Dean's Yard, Westminster Abbey (102); The Palm House, Kew Gardens (109); The tow path, Grand Union Canal, Regent's Park (110); Old St Mary's Churchyard, Stoke Newington Church Street (119); A stallholder, Brick Lane Market (120); The Thames at Putney (129); The Thames from Bermondsey Wall toward Wapping (130); Greenwich Park (141); Battersea Power Station (142); Shoppers in Oxford Street (149); Liverpool Street Station (150); The Thames and Tower Bridge from London Bridge (159).

INTRODUCTION

This is the first anthology of poetry about London. This is surprising since many poets over the centuries have been inspired by London – by its streets, its buildings, its churches, its river, its pubs and, above all, its people.

I have arranged the poems as a tour of London. Apart from two sections on London Weather and London Travel, each section is firmly rooted in a specific topographical area but with some of the boundaries I have used a little poetic licence. I start with the City because that's where London started and then make my way from the North down into the Centre, with a swing out to the West and to the East, before coming to rest across the Thames in South London. I have also dated each poem as closely as I can to show not only how London has changed but also how certain themes, attitudes and impressions have remained remarkably constant over the years.

Can poets do a better job in describing London than the great prose writers like Dr Johnson, Ruskin, Dickens and Virginia Woolf? I think they can. Just look at the vivid description by Swift in 1710 of the behaviour of Londoners when caught in a shower of rain. Or look at Alan Brownjohn's 'Ode to Centre Point'. Volumes have been written about this extraordinary and unlettable building and prosaic invective has rained down upon it, but in a few lines Brownjohn says it all.

Soho, for example, has been described, analysed and photographed a million times, but stroll around it in the company of Gavin Ewart's poem and you'll soon succumb to its colourful and cosmopolitan seediness. In this poem he reaches back to the eighteenth century, for in all of these streets and alleyways there is a strong sense of the continuum of history. You can't escape it in London; the past permeates the present, yet each succeeding present has to live with itself and stamp its individual mark on these London stones.

13

Shona Burns, a new young poet, senses this in her search for a house where she once worked in Highbury:

> that spectral tenement is penned
> in a fold of time with the dead
> and even as I search for its site, its wraith
> has faded, flickered and fled.

Nostalgia is not all. There is a gaiety and liveliness too. I've included three Music Hall songs: 'Burlington Bertie', 'Knock'd 'em in the Old Kent Road' and the imperishable 'If it Wasn't for the 'Ouses in Between' because the gusto of the Victorian Music Hall was rooted in the cheerfulness of the Cockney who in this way was able to triumph over appalling living conditions.

It's no bad thing for people to sing about the place where they live. Only New York and Paris have inspired songs like London. No one seems to want to break out into a verse or two about the joys of Melbourne, Montreal or Madrid. Noel Coward's songs carried on this tradition and his 'London Pride' can lay claim to being London's unofficial anthem. I've also included a lyric by a contemporary songwriter, Ewan MacColl, which describes a journey of two sweethearts from Woolwich Pier to Hampton Court – one which many lovers in London have taken over the ages.

Many of these poems are topographical in that they describe places, but behind them and making them come alive are the people of London. Through the people a poet can capture the spirit of the place. Sir John Betjeman distils the flavour of North London by describing some of the women who choose to live there:

> From the geyser ventilators
> Autumn winds are blowing down
> On a thousand business women
> Having baths in Camden Town.

Jon Stallworthy is prompted by Nelson in Trafalgar Square to reflect upon the people who trod the streets of London and went out from them to make Britain the most powerful nation in the world. Writing in the middle of the Second World War, after London had withstood the Blitz, Ruthven Todd reasserts the essential truth:

14

People are more than places, more than pride;
A million photographs record the works of Wren;
A city remains a city on credit from the tide
That flows among its rocks, a sea of men.

Over the centuries and up and down the social scale the people have made the places, and the places have made the people. There is a relationship, a mutual crediting, an unrecorded interchange between the creator and the created.

Londoners are gregarious. Their great moments of joy are shared whether they are cheering outside Buckingham Palace, dancing in Piccadilly Circus, going to football matches or singing calypsos at Lord's. Pubs were not invented in London but they have an important role in addition to the imbibing of liquor. John Heath-Stubbs, lamenting the death of a pub in Notting Hill, points this out:

> Yet a Public House, perhaps makes manifest also
> the Hidden City; implies its laws
> of tolerance, hierarchy, exchange.

Yes, tolerance. Londoners are tolerant and patient, whether they are waiting for a bus that never seems to come or queueing up for tickets for the Proms. Tolerant, too, of other people. Throughout its history London has welcomed and absorbed many immigrant groups, who've often been the victims of persecution elsewhere. In the 1930s a Jewish immigrant, Avram Stencl, wrote:

> And sacred is Whitechapel
> It is numbered with our Jewish towns.

And in 1980 a young black girl from St Lucia yearns for her old home as she begins to make her new one in Kennington. London has been enriched by these flows of immigrants and indeed today much of the economic activity of the inner city is sustained by Asian families.

These people, those of today and of yesterday, have a sense of belonging. It is no mean city, or as Noel Coward put it:

> This old spot is a bloody good place to be.

This Old Spot
Is A Bloody Good Place
To Be

London Is A Little Bit Of All Right

I was born and bred in London,
It's the only city I know
Though it's foggy and cold and wet
I'd be willing to take a bet
That there ain't no other place I'd want to go....

London – is a little bit of all right,
Nobody can deny that's so,
Big Ben – Bow Bells,
Have a good laugh and watch the swells
Treating themselves to a trot in Rotten Row
Sitting on horses,
Grosvenor Square or Petticoat Lane
Belgravia, Peckham Rye,
You can stray through any neighbourhood,
If you haven't a swanky club
Just pop into the nearest pub,
A little of what you fancy does you good,
And I'd like to mention
London – is a place where you can call right
Round and have a cosy cup of tea,
If you use your loaf a bit and know what's what
This old spot
Is a bloody good place to be.

NOËL COWARD (1963)

London

I am the city of two divided cities
Where the eyes of rich and poor collide and wonder;
Where the beggar's voice is low and unexpectant,
And in clubs the feet of the servants are soft on the carpet
And the world's wind scarcely stirs the leaves of *The Times*.

I am the reticent, the private city,
The city of lovers hiding wrapped in shadows
The city of people sitting and talking quietly
Beyond shut doors and walls as thick as a century,
People who laugh too little and too loudly,
Whose tears fall inward, flowing back to the heart.

I am the city whose fog will fall like a finger gently
Erasing the anger of angles, the strident indecorous gesture,
Whose dusk will come like tact, like a change in the
    conversation,
Violet and indigo, with strings of lemon streetlamps
Casting their pools into the pools of rain
As the notes of the piano are cast from the top-floor
    window
Into the square that is always Sunday afternoon.

A. S. J. TESSIMOND (1938)

London Is A Fine Town

O London is a dainty place,
    A great and gallant city!
For all the Streets are pav'd with gold,
    And all the folks are witty.
And there's your lords and ladies fine,
    That ride in coach and six;
That nothing drink but claret wine,
    And talk of politicks.

And there's your dames with dainty frames,
    With skins as white as milk;
Dressed every day in garments gay,
    Of satin and of silk.
And if your mind be so inclined
    To offer them your arm,
Pull out a handsome purse of gold,
    They can't resist the charm.

STREET BALLAD (1789)

For A London Child
For Jonathan

Sleep where the plane tree nets you with shadow,
A geranium like a lamp at your elbow.

Sleep to the rocking rhythm of trains
To the scent of petunias blooded by June rains.

Sleep by a sea of asphalt, rubbery with heat,
Where people's voices are stones thrown from the street.

Sleep in dreams whose glances are all loving,
Now when the clock is steady, before the hands start
   moving.

Sleep to the query of dogs, muzzles glinting like metal,
Whose own mouth knows only the breast's white milkfall.

Sleep now, wool mariner, on waves of content,
Admiral of innocence, scrutinising and silent.

Sleep where green leaves feather the stone
Urns stained by winter, falling for you alone;

Who wait your first winter, child still cocooned
From cold, a half-sketched poem, mandolin not yet tuned.

Sleep in your image of sailor or poet, explorer, engine-
   driver,
Child of two kisses, on your brow a four-leaved clover.

ALAN ROSS (1967)

To The City of London*

London, thou art of towns the A per se.
Sovereign of cities, seemliest in sight,
Of high renown, riches, and royalty;
Of lords, barons, and many goodly knight;
Of most delectable lusty ladies bright;
Of famous prelates in habits clerical;
Of merchants full of substance and might:
London thou art the flower of cities all. . . .

Strong be thy walls that about thee stands;
Wise be the people that within thee dwells;
Fresh is thy river with his lusty strands;
Blithe be thy churches, well sounding be thy bells;
Rich be thy merchants in substance that excells
Fair be thy wives, right lovesome white and small;
Clear be thy virgins, lusty under kells:
London, thou art the flower of cities all. . . .

WILLIAM DUNBAR (1501)

* These two verses are from one of the earliest poems to celebrate London
– here in its flurry of mercantile, courtly and sexual energy as it entered
the Renaissance. In 1501 the population of London stood at 50,000; by
the death of Elizabeth in 1603 it had risen to 200,000.
(A kell is a covering – thus clothing – or membrane!)

First Impressions

When I came to England
my husband came to meet me.
We took a taxi to the Oval.
When I reached the house
I was looking for the bathroom.
I said, 'Where's the bath?
Where we going to sleep?'
He said to me, 'There's the bed.'
It was all in one room.
The stove and the bed in the same room.
The sink was on the landing.
I had to catch water
and take it to my room to have a wash.
I felt so sad because I missed my mum
and my house in St Lucia.
So two days later I said,
'Can I go home?'
He said to me,
'You must be joking!
We have to stay and work.
When we have money, then we can go back.'

M. S. (1980)

The City

London Mourning In Ashes *

Of Fire, Fire, Fire I sing,
    that have more cause to cry,
In the Great Chamber of the King,
    (a City mounted High;)
Old *London* that,
Hath stood in State,
    above six hundred years,
In six days space,
Woe and alas!
    is burn'd and drown'd in tears.

The second of *September* in
    the middle time of night,
In *Pudding-lane* it did begin,
    to burn and blaze out right;
Where all that gaz'd,
Were so amaz'd,
    at such a furious flame,
They knew not how,
Or what to do
    that might expel the same.

It swallow'd *Fishstreet hil*, & straight
    it lick'd up *Lombard street*,
Down *Canon-street* in blazing State
    it flew with flaming feet;
Down to the *Thames*
Whose shrinking streams,
    began to ebb away,
As thinking that,
The power of Fate
    had brought the latter day. . . .

ANON (1666)

The Foundling

'Twas on a holy Thursday, their innocent faces clean,
The children walking two and two, in red, and blue, and
    green:
Grey-headed beadles walked before, with wands as white as
    snow,
Till into the high dome of St Paul's they like Thames
    waters flow.

O what a multitude they seemed, these flowers of London
    town!
Seated in companies they sit, with radiance all their own.
The hum of multitudes was there, but multitudes of lambs,
Thousands of little boys and girls raising their innocent
    hands.

Now like a mighty wind they raise to heaven the voice of
    song,
Or like harmonious thunderings the seats of heaven among:
Beneath them sit the aged men, wise guardians of the poor.
Then cherish pity, lest you drive an angel from your door.

WILLIAM BLAKE (1789)

The Lord Mayor's Show

How well I remember the ninth of November,
The Sky very foggy, the Sun looking groggy,
In fact, altogether pea-soup colour's weather.
Shop-windows all shutter'd, the pavement all butter'd,
Policemen paraded, the street barricaded,
   And a peal from the steeple of Bow!
Low women in pattens, high ladies in satins,
And Cousin Suburbans, in flame-colour'd turbans,
Quite up to the attics, inviting rheumatics,
A great mob collecting, without much selecting.
And some, it's a pity, are free of the city,
   As your pockets may happen to know! ...

Such hustle and bustle, and mobbing and robbing,
All, all to see the Lord May'r's Show! ...

How well I remember the ninth of November,
The fine Lady May'ress, an Ostrich's heiress,
In best bib and tucker, and dignified pucker,
The learned Recorder, in Old Bailey order,
The Sheriffs together, – with their hanging weather,
   And their heads like John Anderson's pow!
The Aldermen courtly, and looking 'red port'ly,
And buckler and bargemen, with other great large men,
With streamers and banners, held up in odd manners,
A mob running 'arter', to see it by 'vater',
   And the Wharfs popping off as they go! ...

Such hustle and bustle, such mobbing and robbing,
All, all to see the Lord May'r's Show!

                                        THOMAS HOOD (1820)

The City

Business men with awkward hips
And dirty jokes upon their lips,
And large behinds and jingling chains,
And riddled teeth and riddling brains,
And plump white fingers made to curl
Round some anaemic city girl,
And so lend colour to the lives
And old suspicions of their wives.

Young men who wear on office stools
The ties of minor public schools,
Each learning how to be a sinner
And tell 'a good one' after dinner,
And so discover it is rather
Fun to go one more than father.
But father, son and clerk join up
To talk about the Football Cup.

JOHN BETJEMAN (1932)

'Doing Nicely, Thank You'
(*In answer to several kind inquiries from the country and overseas*)

Troy fell. It is not very probable Time will renew it,
   But London remains full of helmeted women and men,
Long tutored in what to do, why, and which way to go to
    it
   And hoping by some means to get to their office by ten.

A city not proud in its heart of heroic performance,
   But slightly bewildered to find that the era of glass
Introduced (I am told) in the days of the conquering
    Normans
   Is now in the night-time of Hitler most likely to pass.

A city that covers with curtains the windowless casement
  And laughs but obeys when the word has come forth
    from the wise
Not to crouch—as they once were enjoined—under beds in
    the basement
  But to leap to the roofs of the buildings and stare at the
    skies.

A city unbroken, unbowed by the threats of the Axis
  And saving a trifle and banting and doing its best
To spare a few coins for the urgent Collector of Taxes
  Who hides with his staff in a funk-hole way down in the
    West.

A city deprived of a part of her principal glories
  Yet still with some monuments standing and some of her
    spires,
And (who shall gainsay me?) how fond of all perilous
    stories!
  How thrilled by the labours of firemen, the watching of
    fires!

A city of painstaking pupils and earnest instructors
  (And everyone's crater the largest of all in the land),
A lemonless, onionless city with female conductors
  On Manchester buses half lost in the wilds of the Strand.

A city if peopled by souls not as stubborn as Cato's,
  Yet facing the bomb-fall (and crowding to look at the
    proofs),
Full-bearded (from shortage of razors), and eating potatoes,
  And standing all night with a sand-bucket up on the
    roofs.

E. V. KNOX (1941)

The Morning After

When the streets are a glimmer of grey
And distances fade from sight,
Then London goes home for the day,
And the bombers come out for the night.

And *Raiders Over* the sirens wail
With a warning, warbling sound,
And down the fire-bombs fall like hail,
And all night long till the east turns pale
The Defiant is hot on the Heinkel's tail
And the sky is a battleground.

The raider keeps hovering over your roof,
And you doubt if your basement is quite bomb-
    proof
As he hums and circles and drones and dives
And whistlers come over your head, in fives,
And was that a bomb or was it a gun?
Is that one of ours now, or is it a Hun?
Here comes a screamer, the end of all!
You can't be hit *if you hear it fall*!
And you're flat on your face with the force of the
    blast
And the whole world's blown to bits.
Then the All Clear signals the *Raiders Passed*,
And dawn is bright in the sky at last,
And you don't find nearly so many hits
The morning after the Blitz.

When darkness dwindles away
The birds of prey take flight,
And London comes out for the day,
And the bombers slink home for the night.

The milk and the postman arrive at the door,
Front doors in the home front-line,
And London stands where it stood before
At work in the bright sunshine.
There's the shiver and tinkle of broken glass,
And here's a corner you cannot pass,
And here's a crater and there's a mine,
And your bus goes round if it can't go through,
Or you've got to walk (and you get there, too)
And girls troop out in the glittering air
With bright spring jackets and turbaned hair,
And if people ask how we carry on
When this is gutted and that is gone,
And face the round of a working day
Trim and jaunty and grim and gay –
Well, Londoners know that they'll be quits
One morning after the Blitz.

SAGITTARIUS (1941)

These Are Facts

These are facts, observe them how you will:
Forget for a moment the medals and the glory,
The clean shape of the bomb, designed to kill,
And the proud headlines of the papers' story.

Remember the walls of brick that forty years
Had nursed to make a neat though shabby home;
The impertinence of death, ignoring tears,
That smashed the house and left untouched the Dome.

Bodies in death are not magnificent or stately,
Bones are not elegant that blast has shattered;
This sorry, stained and crumpled rag was lately
A man whose life was made of little things that
    mattered;

33

Now he is just a nuisance, liable to stink,
A breeding-ground for flies, a test-tube for disease:
Bury him quickly and never pause to think,
What is the future worth to men like these?

People are more than places, more than pride;
A million photographs record the works of Wren;
A city remains a city on credit from the tide
That flows among its rocks, a sea of men.

RUTHVEN TODD (1942)

Tribute to St Paul's

Rising from the embers of the other fire,
The calculated beauty of your dome
Replaced the gothic aspirations of the spire,
Made London rival to Bramante's Rome.

War – and your beauty now a carapace;
Vulnerable what we would most protect;
Anxious, we turned our eyes upon this mass,
This monument to its own architect.

Still, we recall how on those fearful nights
Lit, as triumphant for a victory,
Among the gaunt and gutted satellites
Your radiant outline stood against the sky.

W. J. STRACHAN (1945)

A View of Barbican

Among the chestnut leaves and tombs
Of Bunhill-fields the evening
Laid down its oblique yellow rays,
And from the city's broken side
The angular fungi of our time
Had lifted geometric heads
Over that village of the dead,
The broken bottles and the weeds.

I thought, why are they desolate,
Etched in the débris of this day,
Those flashing headstones that erect
So salt an epitaph to the sky?
Bland oblongs in the fragile sun
Offering no crevice to a bird
And to no living human soul
A nightly habitation,

They watch the excremental flood
Of Thames spill slowly to the sea
Beyond the spar of Stepney spire
And, coming up the other way,
A slower summer evening.
I saw where, also memorial, stood
Beneath those memnons of our day,
A rubric of the Roman wall.

Those ghosts that make a city, they
Lay under leaves, and under stones
A dozen Londons under ground,
While I, among the yellow tombs,
Watch a short wind whirl up the dust,
A wing of yesterday's newspaper
Roll over the macadam road
To wrap itself about a wire;

And the glazed facades everywhere
Guarding bitter rubble and
An anonymity of place
Impose on those who, buried there,
Sleep each his individual sleep;
The common limbo of progress
Builded about the irregular dead;
The anonymity of nowhere.

So well I recognised the scene!
As light retreated into shade,
Both solitude and wilderness!
I thought, as I stood silent then,
How I inhabited no place
As surely as those dead beneath
The derelict sarcophagi
Dwell in a scarcely sadder bed.

DAVID WRIGHT (1965)

A Rose Is Not A Rose

A rose is not a rose

in Our Gardening Correspondent's prose.

Crushed between SPIDERMAN'S ACCIDENT
and OSPREYS NESTING it gives off no scent

to sweeten our commuting breath.
On the walk from the station, with

yesterday's record crop of dead
and a column of births folded

under my arm, I enter
Smithfield where the porters saunter

among carcases. Snout by snout
pigs that the cleaver turned inside out

are hung, drawn and quartered. Parts
I do not recognise loll from carts.

A solitary trotter
blanches as it stains the gutter –

making the eyes recoil, nerves shrink,

Blood is not blood when it is ink.

JON STALLWORTHY (1969)

.

The North,
St Marylebone
and Bloomsbury

Sunday At Hampstead

(An idle idyll by a very humble member of the great and noble London mob)

This is the Heath of Hampstead,
There is the dome of Saint Paul's;
Beneath, on the serried house-tops,
A chequered lustre falls:

And the mighty city of London,
Under the clouds and the light,
Seems a low wet beach, half shingle,
With a few sharp rocks upright.

Here will we sit, my darling,
And dream an hour away:
The donkeys are hurried and worried,
But we are not donkeys to-day:

Through all the weary week, dear,
We toil in the murk down there,
Tied to a desk and a counter,
A patient stupid pair!

But on Sunday we slip our tether,
And away from the smoke and the smirch;
Too grateful to God for His Sabbath
To shut its hours in a church.

Away to the green, green country,
Under the open sky;
Where the earth's sweet breath is incense
And the lark sings psalms on high.

On Sunday we're Lord and Lady,
With ten times the love and glee
Of those pale and languid rich ones
Who are always and never free.

41

They drawl and stare and simper,
So fine and cold and staid,
Like exquisite waxwork figures
That must be kept in the shade:

We can laugh out loud when merry,
We can romp at kiss-in-the-ring,
We can take our beer at a public,
We can loll on the grass and sing. . . .

Would you grieve very much, my darling,
If all yon low wet shore
Were drowned by a mighty flood-tide,
And we never toiled there more?

JAMES THOMPSON (1880)

The Fields From Islington*

The fields from Islington to Marylebone,
To Primrose Hill and Saint John's Wood,
Were builded over with pillars of gold,
And there Jerusalem's pillars stood.
            Her little-ones ran on the fields,
            The Lamb of God among them seen,
            And Fair Jerusalem his Bride,
            Among the little meadows green.
Pancras and Kentish-town repose
Among her golden pillars high,
Among her golden arches which,
Shine upon the starry sky.
            The Jew's-Harp House and the Green Man
            The Ponds where Boys to bathe delight,
            The Fields of Cows by Willan's farm,
            Shine in Jerusalem's pleasant sight. . . .

What are those golden Builders doing
near mournful ever-weeping Paddington,
Standing above the mighty Ruin
Where Satan the first victory won,
      Where Albion slept beneath the Fatal Tree,
      and the Druids' golden knife
      Rioted in human gore,
      In offerings of Human Life?
They groaned aloud on London Stone,
They groaned aloud on Tyburn's Brook,
Albion gave his deadly groan,
And all the Atlantic Mountains shook, ...

WILLIAM BLAKE (1804–1820)   from *Jerusalem*

★ At the end of the eighteenth century there was a great surge of land
development in North London. Somers Town was developed by Lord
Somers; Camden Town on fields owned by Lord Chancellor Camden;
Paddington on the farms owned by the Bishop of London; and the Eyre
family built the villas of St John's Wood where men of fashion kept their
mistresses.

March Morning, N.W.3

The fields from Islington to Marylebone,
To Primrose Hill and Saint John's Wood,
Were builded over with pillars of gold,
And there Jerusalem's pillars stood.
               WILLIAM BLAKE

A wind that rocked the stems of cranes
and daffodils across the park
snapped the bedroom curtains
in my face, and drills broke up the dark.

Time to step up from underground
time to step out and take the air,
blood whispered, tired of tracking round
that unlit inner circle where

the living ride with the dead
and those now neither who will
be both. The March sun overhead,
turning the tide in vein and tendril,

turned me out of doors; turned my feet
from the pinstripe parallels
of a straight and narrow street
to the path over Primrose Hill.

Fountainheads, sealed with soot, answered
the sun, and I saw their green lips
opened again. Root and bole stirred
to a new pulse bending twig-tips

skyward, building the intricate
cities of summer from a blue-
print of spring. It was half past eight
by the ever-right sun. Below

me London sloughed its winter skin,
smoke coiling westward; to the east
window-scales were golden. In
that moment the snarling drills ceased

and a voice lassooed me. Daffodil-
yellow his helmet, twenty floors high,
he stood on a scaffolding grill
waving a cloud to catch my eye.

And I waved my handkerchief back
(hearing no word of his message
for the drills were ploughing tarmac
again; a terrace's wreckage

turned to a bulldozer's breakfast).
Was he asking the time, mocking
the shine on my trowsers, or just
wishing me luck? *Time to be making*

44

a fresh start, boyo, I wanted
to say. *Watch how the plane-trees hoist
into leaf the distilled dead –
this year's leaf higher than last.*

*The graveyards of London renew
the middle air; our province; soon
to be theirs, who through nerve circuits now
signal to be hoisted to the sun.*

JON STALLWORTHY (1969)

Business Girls

From the geyser ventilators
    Autumn winds are blowing down
On a thousand business women
    Having baths in Camden Town.

Waste pipes chuckle into runnels,
    Steam's escaping here and there,
Morning trains through Camden cutting
    Shake the Crescent and the Square.

Early nip of changeful autumn,
    Dahlias glimpsed through garden doors,
At the back precarious bathrooms
    Jutting out from upper floors,

And behind their frail partitions
    Business women lie and soak,
Seeing through the draughty skylight
    Flying clouds and railway smoke.

Rest you there, poor unbelov'd ones,
    Lap your loneliness in heat.
All too soon the tiny breakfast,
    Trolley-bus and windy street!

JOHN BETJEMAN (1954)

The Canal From Camden Town To Duncan Terrace

purple duck
with long wooden wings
V in the water
dimpled, dipped

somewhere in a city
corrugated water winds
rising and falling
at plump locks

an Albion boat
narrows past Jericho
a black dog
sparks
at the water

autumn Sunday
hurried us out to walk
the new-planked concrete path
scurries us back
past
quilted water
rain-stippled

look up at the skies
through windows vaulting
the air
past men
swearing at double time

past the black dog
now happy on grass
we hug our coats
and look forward to tea

MICHELENE WANDOR (1981)

Phantom

I've lived in this corner of Highbury now
for fifteen years or more
and I've gradually come to remember
that I had been here before.
I had had a job as a typist once
in a tall house, gloomy grey,
and I've searched for that house down the living
    streets
but it's crumbled clean away.

As sure as I walk the familiar streets
that house stood somewhere here
but the map is deranged or the scene has changed
and the streets wear a different air.
That spectral tenement is penned
in a fold of time with the dead
and even as I search for its site, its wraith
has faded, flickered, and fled.

SHONA BURNS (1981)

Regent's Park Zoo

Not on the side of the angels, I keep
words in cheek pouches, and lead apes
in hell. I look into your eyes
through bars; dead trees and wire cages
you hang upon, your long tails curled,
and your sad faces wrinkled, just the clasp
of a hand away, a half-bitten grape
dropped on the floor, and the door
locked from the inside.

47

All around young mothers walk in jeans,
their babies slung in canvas straps,
a trendy habit as ancient as the small
monkey clamped to a teat, demand feeding.
The crowds wander aimlessly, free
in their larger cage, and have paid
an entrance fee, will pay at last
a bigger debt than this in offices
and homes tomorrow.

Soft fur, bare arses, hair styles
like rock groups, the apes look intelligent,
but bare teeth in sudden warning.
The people bare theirs in quick smiles
or laugh aloud to see themselves gibber
on the other side. So far I have not
seen men beating hairy chests,
but it will come. Meanwhile they make
bombs and grunt at love.

A young zoo-keeper, decent, clean
and infinitely kind, puts a scrubbed hand
into theirs, shovels out their food,
or offers an over-ripe banana. Some
fling their arms about his sunburnt neck,
purse up their lips as if about to kiss,
but defecate where and when they please.
(Nappies are reserved for domestic chimpanzees.)
Closing time. Open up the cage.

ELIZABETH BARTLETT (1981)

Victory Calypso, Lord's 1950

Cricket, lovely cricket,
At Lord's where I saw it;
Cricket, lovely cricket,
At Lord's where I saw it;
Yardley tried his best
But Goddard won the test.
They gave the crowd plenty fun;
Second Test and West Indies won.

With those two little pals of mine
Ramadhin and Valentine. . . .

The King was there well attired,
So they started with Rae and Stollmeyer;
Stolly was hitting balls around the boundary,
But Wardle stopped him at twenty.
Rae had confidence,
So he put up a strong defence;
He saw the King was waiting to see,
So he gave him a century.

With those two little pals of mine
Ramadhin and Valentine. . . .

West Indies was feeling homely,
Their audience had them happy.
When Washbrook's century had ended,
West Indies' voices all blended.
Hats went in the air.
They jumped and shouted without fear;
So at Lord's was the scenery
Bound to go down in history.

After all was said and done,
Second Test and West Indies won!

EGBERT MOORE ('LORD BEGINNER')

49

Post Office Tower

The bloodshot eyes blink,
Across the green crystal roofs
Of the British Museum, over
The grey fortress of the grim
Senate House, above the black
Bloomsbury chimneys silhouetted
Like saw-teeth on the timber-pale sky
And through the dark serrated wings
Of the wind-worried sumachs
Which shake against the gleaming afterglow.

The bloodshot eyes blink,
Burning eyes, red for danger
Eyes but not frightening eyes
Because their movement is as
Reassuring and regular as the tick
Of an alarm clock set for tomorrow.
This mechanical clown, unreal
As a dalek, harmless as a horror film,
Is silent and stationary, does not
Worry me and never disturbs my sleep.

The bloodshot eyes blink.
Less sinister than the weird
Pair of green window-eyes
In the dome of the Reading Room,
Less lethal looking than the yellow
Unblinking eyes on the giant cranes
Which watch me from Warren Street,
Comic eyes because they make this monster look
Like some helter-skelter ride, some lighted-up
Surprise, newly arrived on a fair ground.

TOM EARLEY (1975)

The British Museum Reading Room

Under the hive-like dome the stooping haunted readers
Go up and down the alleys, tap the cells of knowledge –
    Honey and wax, the accumulation of years –
Some on commission, some for the love of learning,
Some because they have nothing better to do
Or because they hope these walls of books will deaden
    The drumming of the demon in their ears.

Cranks, hacks, poverty-stricken scholars,
In pince-nez, period hats or romantic beards
    And cherishing their hobby or their doom
Some are too much alive and some are asleep
Hanging like bats in a world of inverted values,
Folded up in themselves in a world which is safe and silent:
    This is the British Museum Reading Room.

Out on the steps in the sun the pigeons are courting,
Puffing their ruffs and sweeping their tails or taking
    A sun-bath at their ease
And under the totem poles – the ancient terror –
Between the enormous fluted Ionic columns
There seeps from heavily jowled or hawk-like foreign faces
    The guttural sorrow of the refugees.

                    LOUIS MacNEICE (July, 1939)

51

Oxford Street, Holborn,
The Strand, Trafalgar Square

St James's And St Giles's*

To the tourist of London who's curious in facts,
I'll point out some things in the principal tracts.
Two places there are where the poor and the rich
Live so like each other, there's no telling which.
One parish, St James's, *par excellence* call'd,
The West end of town and the fashionable world;
The other St Giles's, if true rumour speaks,
Is inhabited solely by Emigrant Greeks.

So don't be astonished at what I shall say,
St James and St Giles I have seen in my day,
In the former they live on the National Debt,
In the latter they live on what they can get. . . .

In St James's they keep up their spirits with wine,
In St Giles's they're drunk on 'blue ruin' by nine.
In St James's they banquet on Silver in state,
In St Giles's the same with a twopenny plate.
In St James's the Officers mess at their Club,
In St Giles's they often have messes for grub;
In St James's they feed on the highest of game,
In St Giles's they live on foul *air* just the same.

ANON (nineteenth century)

* This street ballad contrasts the affluent comfort and wealth of St James's,
the heart of clubland (which still exists), with the drunken squalor and
poverty of St Giles. St Giles was demolished by the extension of New
Oxford Street but for centuries it had been a slum and it was the scene
for Hogarth's famous drawing of Gin Alley.

Ode to Centre Point*

One of the most
Paradoxical of infertil
　　-ity symbols
Lately contrived, a vast
　　Barren phallus of
Egg-boxes without eggs, it
　　Simultaneously wav
-ers and maintains its own
　　Projection into the
Soft depths of the sky, a
　　Thing of monumental
Insignificance, making no
　　Impression and
Quite ignorable, unless for
　　its huge vac
-uity. But in so rapidly
　　Appearing, it rased out
Everything lively on its site:
　　Small blocks of
Usefully inhabited mansion
　　Flats, various
Helpful shops, a passable
　　Ristorante, an
Experimental theatre, and
　　All of the navigable
Pavement on one side of the
　　Charing Cross Road,
Substituting, at ground level, a
　　Blue pond inside
Crass concrete walls with square
　　-Fingered fountains jetting
The water; and above, shooting upward
　　A weird, implacable
Cliff of patterned stone, glass and
　　Air, a hive of empty
Cells, tilting, apparently, as the
　　Clouds above pass over,

And at one dizzying, approximate
        Count, thirty-three stories high.
Therefore, it impinges on us all,
        Notwithstanding, and needs
To be taken into account; which
        Is why strong men with de
-termination and research have
        Gone grey trying to
Discover why it is there
        (But then who, exactly,
Wanted and actually willed Shell
        Mex or the Euston Road?). . . .

ALAN BROWNJOHN (1972)

*Centre Point in St Giles Circus at the bottom of Tottenham Court
Road is a block of offices and flats rising to a height some twenty feet
taller than St Paul's. It was built by the property developer, Harry
Hyams, in 1966 but it remained empty for several years. It became the
symbol of the most unacceptable in the property boom, since its value
rose dramatically in spite of it being unlet. Camden Council failed to
acquire it by compulsory purchase order in 1972 and in 1974 it was
occupied by a group protesting against property speculation. It remained
virtually unlet until the CBI took a large part of it in 1979 but they in
their turn found it difficult to meet the high rate demands of Camden
Council.

Coming Up Oxford Street: Evening

The sun from the west glares back,
And the sun from the watered track,
And the sun from the sheets of glass,
And the sun from each window-brass;
Sun-mirrorings, too, brighten
From show-cases beneath
The laughing eyes and teeth
Of ladies who rouge and whiten.
And the same warm god explores
Panels and chinks of doors;
Problems with chymists' bottles
Profound as Aristotle's
He solves, and with good cause,
Having been ere man was.

Also he dazzles the pupils of one who walks west,
A city-clerk, with eyesight not of the best,
Who sees no escape to the very verge of his days
From the rut of Oxford Street into open ways;
And he goes along with head and eyes flagging forlorn,
Empty of interest in things, and wondering why he was
    born.

THOMAS HARDY (4 July, 1872)

Celia Celia

When I am sad and weary
When I think all hope has gone
When I walk along High Holborn
I think of you with nothing on

ADRIAN MITCHELL (1968)

58

Footnotes on Celia Celia

Used to slouch along High Holborn
in my gruesome solo lunch-hours.
It was entirely lined
with Gothick insurance offices
except for one oblong block of a shop
called Gamages,
where, once,
drunk, on Christmas Eve,
I bought myself a battery-operated Japanese pig
with a chef's hat on top of his head
and a metal stove which lit up red
and the pig moved a frying pan up and down with his hand
and tossed a plastic fried egg into the air
and caught it again the other way up
and then tossed it and caught it again and again
all the time emitting squeals of excitement
through a series of holes in the top of his head –

but apart from that . . . I want to forget High Holborn.

ADRIAN MITCHELL (1975)

Fleet Street

From north and south, from east and west,
Here in one shrieking vortex meet
These streams of life, made manifest
Along the shaking quivering street.
Its pulse and heart that throbs and glows
As if strife were its repose.

I shut my ear to such rude sounds
As reach a harsh discordant note,
Till, melting into what surrounds,
My soul doth with the current float,
And from the turmoil and the strife
Wakes all the melody of life.

The stony buildings blankly stare
While murder's being done within,
While man returns his fellow's glare
The secrets of his soul to miss.
And each man's heart is foul with lust
Of women, or the blind gold dust.

ISAAC ROSENBERG (1906)

1930

Eating a Lyons' chop in nineteen thirty,
And staring through the heavy-lidded pane,
Wondering why they keep their plates so dirty,
And why there's dust in a London April rain,
I shall see out of the sick swim of faces,
Huddled beneath umbrellas in the Strand,
Dim reminiscence of those bitter places,
Where my rich cargo drove upon the sand.

Then through the crumbling of some bread I'll ponder,
I'll ponder through the scraping of a plate,
How love which should have been a blaze of wonder,
Has been a dusty and untended grate,
With crooked, grimy bars twisted asunder,
Because its servant rose from sleep too late.

GRAHAM GREENE

Burlington Bertie From Bow*

I'm Bert
P'raps you've heard of me
Bert
You've had word of me
Jogging along
Hearty and strong
Living on plates of fresh air.
I dress up in fashion, and, when I'm feeling depress'd
I shave from my cuff
All the whiskers and fluff,
Stick my hat on and toddle up West.

I'm Burlington Bertie
I rise at ten thirty
And saunter along like a toff.
I walk down the Strand
With my gloves on my hand,
Then I walk down again with them off.
I'm all airs and graces, correct easy paces,
Without food so long I've forgot where my face is.
I'm Bert, Bert, I haven't a shirt,
But my people are well off you know!
Nearly everyone knows me from Smith to Lord Roseb'ry
I'm Burlington Bertie from Bow! . . .

My pose,
Tho' ironical
Shows
That my monocle
Holds up my face
Keeps it in place,
Stops it from slipping away.
Cigars I smoke thousands, I usually deal in the Strand,
But you've got to take care
When you're getting them there
Or some idiot might stand on your hand.

I'm Burlington Bertie
I rise at ten thirty
Then Buckingham Palace I view.
I stand in the Yard
While they're changing the Guard
And the King shouts across 'Toodle oo'.
The Prince of Wales' brother, along with some other,
Slaps me on the back, and says, 'Come round and see
    Mother'.
I'm Bert, Bert and Royalty's hurt
When they ask me to dine, I say 'No'!
'I've just had a banana with Lady Diana
'I'm Burlington Bertie from Bow!'

WILLIAM HARGREAVES (1915)

★ This was sung by Ella Shields, the famous male impersonator.

Room 28
National Portrait Gallery, London

Remembered as octagonal, dark-panelled,
    And seldom frequented, except by me –
        Indeed, a bower
Attained down avenues where, framed and annalled,
    Great England's great with truculence outlive
        Their hour
And, pigmented, endure mean immortality –
    The room gave rest as some libraries give.

The visitor, approaching, brushed a girlish
    Bust of Lord Byron. Sir James George Frazer's head,
        An unarmed sentry,
Austere, tormented, brazen-browed, and churlish,
    Guarded with sternness fit for Stygian gates
        The entry
To harmless walls where men of letters lately dead
    Were hung. The envied spot was held by Yeats.

His mask, alone a mask among the paintings,
  Attracted to itself what little sun
    The sky admitted.
Half-bronze, half-black, his Janus-face at matins
  Amazed that dim arena of the less
    Weird-witted
Survivors of a blurred time: presbyters upon
  Whose faces grieved the ghost of Earnestness.

The whites of Rider Haggard's eyes were showing
  When last I saw them. Conrad's cheeks were green,
    And Rudyard Kipling's
Pink profile burned against his brown works, glowing
  With royalties and realism. Fine
    Sweet stipplings
Limned the long locks that Ellen Terry, seventeen,
  Pre-Raphaelite, and blonde, let down to shine.

There Stevenson looked ill and ill-depicted;
  Frail Patmore, plucked yet gamey; Henry James,
    Our good grammarian,
More paunched and politic than I'd expected.
  Among the lone-faced portraits loomed a trin-
    Itarian
Composite: Baring, Chesterton, Belloc. The frame's
  Embellished foursquare dogma boxed them in.

Brave room! Where are they now? In college courses,
  Perused in inferior light, then laid
    On library tables.
Green knights mismounted on empirical horses,
  Encumbered by old armor and a heraldry
    Of labels,
Their universe did not deserve their vows. They fade
  In pale sun, at rest in neither century.

JOHN UPDIKE (1957)

Hot Day In The National Gallery
after Sassoon

Everyone suddenly started taking their clothes off,
The ladies in hats and the girls in leather,
And one girl started scratching herself,
And when people started feeling each other
In front of the Rubens and the Piero di Cosimos
The attendants were mute.

Nobody told the police, because of the spontaneity, when
Everyone impulsively fell in love in the National Gallery
And started doing everything artists had only dreamed
    about,

As if they were all in celestial bodies on the Astral Plane
Or bacchanaling around in the Elysian Fields,
With the sun shafting in through the dome,
Catching water, making wine.

HERBERT LOMAS (1974)

Epilogue To An Empire
1600–1900
An Ode For Trafalgar Day

As I was crossing Trafalgar Square
whose but the Admiral's shadow hand
should tap my shoulder. At my ear:
'You Sir, stay-at-home citizen
poet, here's more use for your pen
than picking scabs. Tell them in England
this: when first I stuck my head in the air,

'winched from a cockpit's tar and blood
to my crow's nest over London, I
looked down on a singular crowd
moving with the confident swell
of the sea. As it rose and fell
every pulse in the estuary
carried them quayward, carried them seaward.

'Box-wallah, missionary, clerk,
lancer, planter, I saw them all
linked like the waves on the waves embark.
Their eyes looked out – as yours look in –
to harbour names on the cabin-
trunks carrying topees to Bengal,
maxims or gospels to lighten a dark

'continent. Blatant as the flag
they went out under were the bright
abstractions nailed to every mast.
Sharpshooters since have riddled most
and buried an empire in their rags –
scrivener, do you dare to write
a little 'e' in the epilogue

'to an empire that spread its wings
wider than Rome? They are folded,
you say, with the maps and flags; awnings
and verandahs overrun
by impis of the ant; sun-
downers sunk, and the planters' blood
turned tea or siphoned into rubber saplings.

'My one eye reports that their roads
remain, their laws, their language
seeding all winds. They were no gods
from harnessed clouds, as the islanders
thought them, nor were they monsters
but men, as you stooped over your page
and you and you and these wind-driven crowds

'are and are not. For you have lost
their rhythm, the pulse of the sea
in their salt blood. Your heart has missed
the beat of centuries, its channels
silted to their source. The muscles
of the will stricken by distrophy
dishonour those that bareback rode the crest

'of untamed seas. Acknowledge
their energy. If you condemn
their violence in a violent age
speak of their courage. Mock their pride
when, having built as well, in as wide
a compass, you have none. Tell them
in England this.'
$$\text{And a pigeon sealed the page.}$$

JON STALLWORTHY (1968)

WHAT JENNER SAID ON HEARING IN ELYSIUM THAT COMPLAINTS HAD BEEN MADE OF HIS HAVING A STATUE IN TRAFALGAR SQUARE

England's ingratitude still blots
The scutcheon of the brave and free;
I saved you from a million spots,
And now you grudge a spot to me.

ANON (1850)

The statues in Trafalgar Square are rather a rum collection, apart from the centre piece. Edward Jenner, the pioneer of vaccination, fortunately didn't get in. There is a large empty plinth at the North East corner, which rumour says is reserved for an equestrian statue of our present queen.

66

St Martin-in-the-Fields

City churches aren't always easy
To pray in: there may be someone buffing brasses
Squeakily, insistently, with cheesy
Breath and a polish of rage behind their glasses,
Sending almost tangible meditations
To disturb our straggly congregations.

Or visitors delicately boggle at the faithful patients,
Guide Book in hand, not expecting religion
In architecture like this. Outside, the pigeons
Drop little pats of white on assembled nations;
Inside we pray, uneasily wondering:
Whoever it is up there, is he listening?

Yet here bums in a blue-chinned Greek-looking worshipper,
Pockets stuffed with evening newspapers, coat
Flapping, and grabs his God by the throat:
He prays precipitately, wagging his head – a pew-gripper
Pointing out to an old employer – what?
Is it horses? A tip flopped? A reproach? Or not?

And suddenly I'm in it: his grace has snatched
Me out: over the altar the angels' faces
Break the wood: they're reaching down with fact,
Listening, embracing, swooping, and I'm hatched:
A broad white shell of completeness
Has widened and cracked:
I'm open to sweetness.

HERBERT LOMAS (1981)

Piccadilly, Soho, Buckingham Palace

London At Night[*]

When summer twilight fades away
And darkness falls and night begins
There ends another dusty day
With all its dreary disciplines
That have tied us to
The work we do
Until the evening gives us ease
To wander for an hour or two
Beneath our London trees. . . .

London at night
With the gas lamps alight
Is renowned for its moral fragility
From ornate, sedate Pall Mall
To the dark romance of Regent's Canal.
Girls in large hats
Outside Boodle's and Pratt's
Lie in wait for the younger nobility
And they frequently compel
Some inebriated swell
To hop into a hansom
And shout through the transom,
'Drive home – drive home like hell!'
Men who survive
Piccadilly alive
And can take the air
In Leicester Square
And not be put to flight
Earnestly say
That Port Said and Bombay
Are a great deal more prim and upright
Than London at night.

NOËL COWARD (1954)
from *After The Ball*

[*]This was written in the 1950s to evoke the world of London in the 1890s.

71

Piccadilly Circus*

Piccadilly Circus
    glows
at the world's heart,
    a midnight rose.

And what in all
    her beauty stirs
under the moon
    her worshippers?

What is her message?
    Line by line
the simple read
    who seek a sign:

Omnia ab uno disce!
    Man shall his salvation
        win,
either by old Shetland
        whiskey
    or through Martin's
        London Gin.

HUMBERT WOLFE (1930)
from *The Uncelestial City*)

---

* At the beginning of the eighteenth century a certain Robert Baker, who was a shirtmaker in the Strand, bought one and a half acres north of the Haymarket in order to build a house. His business was making high collars for the bucks which were called *pickadils*, and his customers christened his house 'Pickadilly Hall'.

V.J. Day

My No. 19, wedged in at the Circus,
Halted beside the Eros pedestal
Still boarded over. Dusty sunlight flickered.
A flutter of torn paper drifted from
The windows of some fourth-floor offices.
The armistice, I guessed; we'd had the bomb;
War's over, so must be celebrated.
En route to somewhere far down Fulham Road
I got off before the World's End, time in hand,
So turned into the nearest.

Old crazies singing Knees up Mother Brown,
A world that even then I knew had ended.
Knees up, arms linked, the floor of the bar parlour
Bounding! Ports and lemon, bombazine!
And all you ladies dead now!

DAVID WRIGHT (1945)

Soho

Eighteenth-Century houses. Neat. Reasonable.
Three streets in alphabetical order
(Reading from West to East):
Dean, Frith and Greek.

Dryden in Gerrard Street, Mozart in Frith,
Prodigious infant. Johnson at the Turk's Head.

But look in Soho Square, the 'stately quadrate'
(A windmill turning then in Rathbone Place).
First resident: Monmouth. Lucifer that fell.

In a more lucid day
This was the heart of fashionable London –
With link boys, chariots, ombre, whist and tea.

73

Routs. Public Assemblies
Of the Nobility and Gentry.
Mrs Cornelys. Carlisle House. Casanova.
The pleasant titillation of (masked) balls,
The flaming candles, Chippendale Chinese.
And at the gates the rough unlettered mob
Ready to throw the old four-letter words.

Now a few only of the first remain,
The original houses. Cowed and small
Beside competitors. These parvenus
Disdain that world of wit and cultured charm,
The pearls of wisdom. The world of Commerce
Is *their* oyster.

This is the architecture dedicated to the proposition
That all that matters is to show a profit.
And on the Soho houses that remain
From that Augustan Age are signs
Of the times. Neon invitations
To eat, drink, watch the girls strip,
Outraging modesty of mild façade.

The streets are full of Mediterranean life,
Italians, Greeks and Cypriots, Maltese,
With Huguenot-descended French.
And, as exotic, furtive blooming, BOOKSHOPS.
For here, before the deluge of the Act,
The connoisseurs bought 'doubles' – 'singles' too,
The happy snaps that could debauch the eye
Of schoolboys, sadists, or the very queer.

And still the trade in flesh continues here,
The warm, compliant flesh that knows no Law,
– but more discreetly. (Every kind of lust
Is more a kind of love than Judges think.)
And on the notice boards tarts' cards proclaim
A change of language, not a change of heart:

ACCOMMODATION
FOR GENTLEMEN ONLY, YOUNG LADY SEEKS
INTERESTING OCCUPATION, even PRIVATE STRIPTEASE.
Below, the cryptic cyphers only the dial fully understands.
Telephone numbers! magic in their power
To serve the twentieth century's good time myth,
The talismans of Northern businessmen.

Less modest once, such cards had photographs,
Vital statistics, and the hidden words
That called the initiates to the Mysteries.
Rainwear. High heels. Bondage. Correction. All
Like jungle drums to lonely fetishists
And those whose impulse learned to deviate.
And this is still a jungle, where at night
The infantile desires may roam at will
With Tarquin's ravishing strides.
Here, in the glistening rain, the mac men come;
A pack of masochists each night whipped in,
Slaves of the 'models' with the hunting crops.

Crooks, ponces, whores. You think: a world away
From eighteenth-century elegance and charm?
The wise (or cynical) have leave to doubt.

GAVIN EWART (1964)

I Went To The Jazz Club

I went to the Jazz Club.
Young over-amplified men played Saxophones
They played very fast –
Perhaps they had a bus to catch?
The drummer played very loud,
Was he deaf?
They were very accomplished musicians
The music didn't touch me
I couldn't hear the tune for the noise.

75

'It's not in here' said an old man.
'I'll show you where.'
He took me to an old house,
Dust lay thick on forgotten chairs.
In the corner was an embalmed piano
The old man raised the lid and pointed.
'It's in there' he said.

SPIKE MILLIGAN (1974)

Night At No 10*

How true it is that London never sleeps!
The traffic's hum might be a lullaby
But for the homing aeroplane, which sweeps
Whining and thundering across the sky.

Each quarter-hour the faithful clocks chime out
With Big Ben flatly bringing up the rear;
And ships hoot on the river, revellers shout,
And even through my dreaming, I can hear

Back-firing cars, and an illegal horn;
And here in Central London, dogs still bark,
While all night long, like heralds of the dawn
The Chinese geese are honking in the Park!

MARY WILSON (1970)

---

* Mrs Wilson spent eight years in all trying to sleep at No 10 Downing Street, a residence which has housed more insomniacs than poets. Rosebery had to be driven around London all night in his primrose carriage to get some sleep. Most Prime Ministers complain about the sound of the bands and the early morning military rehearsals on Horse Guards Parade.

Buckingham Palace

They're changing guard at Buckingham Palace –
Christopher Robin went down with Alice.
Alice is marrying one of the guard.
'A soldier's life is terrible hard,'
Says Alice.

They're changing guard at Buckingham Palace –
Christopher Robin went down with Alice.
We saw a guard in a sentry-box.
'One of the sergeants looks after their socks,'
Says Alice.

They're changing guard at Buckingham Palace –
Christopher Robin went down with Alice.
We looked for the King, but he never came.
'Well, God take care of him, all the same,'
Says Alice.

They're changing guard at Buckingham Palace –
Christopher Robin went down with Alice.
They've great big parties inside the grounds.
'I wouldn't be King for a hundred pounds,'
Says Alice.

They're changing guard at Buckingham Palace –
Christopher Robin went down with Alice.
A face looked out, but it wasn't the King's.
'He's much too busy a-signing things,'
Says Alice.

They're changing guard at Buckingham Palace –
Christopher Robin went down with Alice.
'Do you think the King knows all about *me*?'
'Sure to, dear, but it's time for tea,'
Says Alice.

A. A. MILNE (1924)

Interlude:

London Weather
and
London Travel

LONDON WEATHER

Fog[★]

Serene and unafraid of solitude,
I worked the short days out, – and watched the sun
On lurid morns or monstrous afternoons...
Push out through fog with his dilated disk,
And startle the slant roofs and chimney-pots
With splashes of fierce colour. Or I saw
Fog only, the great tawny weltering fog
Involve the passive city, strangle it
Alive, and draw it off into the void,
Spires, bridges, streets, and squares, as if a sponge
Had wiped out London, – or as noon and night
Had clapped together and utterly struck out
The intermediate time, undoing themselves
In the act. Your city poets see such things ...
But sit in London at the day's decline,
And view the city perish in the mist
Like Pharaoh's armaments in the deep Red Sea,
The chariots, horsemen, footmen, all the host,
Sucked down and choked to silence – then, surprised
By a sudden sense of vision and of tune,
You feel as conquerors though you did not fight ....

ELIZABETH BARRATT BROWNING (1856)
from *Aurora Leigh*

★ The famous fogs of London were known as 'pea-soupers' or 'London Particulars'. The Clean Air Act, which outlawed the burning of coal, stopped these great fogs in the 1960s. This was good for bronchitis, but bad for romance. There was a strange fascination in a London Particular. Once I walked in front of my wife's car holding a torch from Westminster Abbey to Chelsea.

81

The Great Frost*

...O Roving Muse, recall that wondrous year
When winter reign'd in bleak Britannia's air;
When hoary Thames, with frosted osiers crown'd,
Was three long moons in icy fetters bound.
The waterman, forlorn along the shore,
Pensive reclines upon his useless oar,
Sees harness'd steeds desert the stony town
And wander roads unstable, not their own;
Wheels o'er the harden'd waters smoothly glide,
And rase with whiten'd tracks the slipp'ry tide.
Here the fat cook piles high the blazing fire,
And scarce the spit can turn the steer entire.
Booths sudden hide the Thames, long streets appear,
And numerous games proclaim the crowded fair.
So when a general bids the martial train
Spread their encampment o'er the spacious plain,
Thick rising tents a canvas city build,
And the loud dice resound thro' all the field.

JOHN GAY (1716)
from *Trivia*

* Old London Bridge, which was not destroyed until 1825, restricted the flow of the river so much that in severe winters it froze over. The Great Frosts were in 1684, 1698 and 1740. Gay does not exaggerate. John Evelyn noted in his diary, 'Coaches plied from Westminster to the Temple and from several other stairs to and fro, as in the streets, sleds, sliding with skates, a bull-baiting, horse and coach races, puppet plays and interludes, cooks, tippling and other lewd places, so that it seemed to be a Bacchanalian triumph, or carnival on the water.'

This piece is from a long poem on the delights of working in London.

Smelling The End Of Green July

Smelling the end of green July
I entered through spiked-gates a London park
To grill my body in the sun,
And to untie thought's parcel of pure dark
Under the blue gaze of the candid sky.

The air was heavy, without breath;
The asphalt paths gave off a hollow ring;
And wearing haloes of shrill birds
The statues watched the flowers withering,
And leaves curl up for Summer's rusty death.

O zoo-like sameness of all parks!
The grasses lick the railings of wrought-iron,
And chains clink in the shrubbery
As Summer roaring like a shabby lion
Claws at the meaning of the human marks.

I saw the tops of buses wheel
Geranium flashes over pigeon-walls;
And heard the rocket-cries of children
Fly upwards, bursting where the water calls,
And scissors sunlight with a glint of steel.

The wings of slowly dripping light
Pulled boats across a swan-enlightened lake;
And near youth's skipping-ropes of joy
I felt the strings of my old parcel break,
Spilling its cold abstractions with delight.

I watched the games of life begun
Among dead matches, droppings of the birds;
And left thought's parcel on a bench
While I relearned the flight of singing words
Under the blowlamp kisses of the sun.

PETER YATES (1950)

London Snow

When men were all asleep the snow came flying,
In large white flakes falling on the city brown,
Stealthily and perpetually settling and loosely lying,
    Hushing the latest traffic of the drowsy town;
Deadening, muffling, stifling its murmurs failing;
Lazily and incessantly floating down and down:
    Silently sifting and veiling road, roof and railing;
Hiding difference, making unevenness even,
Into angles and crevices softly drifting and sailing.
    All night it fell, and when full inches seven
It lay in the depth of its uncompacted lightness,
The clouds blew off from a high and frosty heaven;
    And all woke earlier for the unaccustomed brightness
Of the winter dawning, the strange unheavenly glare:
The eye marvelled – marvelled at the dazzling whiteness;
    The ear hearkened to the stillness of the solemn air;
No sound of wheel rumbling nor of foot falling,
And the busy morning cries came thin and spare.
    Then boys I heard, as they went to school, calling,
They gathered up the crystal manna to freeze
Their tongues with tasting, their hands with snowballing;
    Or rioted in a drift, plunging up to the knees;
Or peering up from under the white-mossed wonder,
'O look at the trees!' they cried, 'O look at the trees!'
    With lessened load a few carts creak and blunder,
Following along the white deserted way,
A country company long dispersed asunder:
    When now already the sun, in pale display
Standing by Paul's high dome, spread forth below
His sparkling beams, and awoke the stir of the day. . . .

ROBERT BRIDGES (1878)

A City Shower – October 1710*

Careful observers may fortell the hour
(By sure prognosticks) when to dread a shower:
While rain depends, the pensive cat gives o'er
Her frolicks, and pursues her tail no more.

86

Returning home at night, you'll find the sink
Strike your offended sense with double stink.
If you be wise, then go not far to dine,
You'll spend in coach-hire more than save in wine.
A coming shower your shooting corns presage,
Old aches throb, your hollow tooth will rage.
Saunt'ring in coffee-house is Dulman seen;
He damns the climate and complains of spleen. . . .
Now in contiguous drops the flood comes down,
Threat'ning with deluge this devoted Town.
To shops in crowds the dogged females fly,
Pretend to cheapen goods, but nothing buy.
The templer spruce, while ev'ry spout's a-broach,
Stays till 'tis fair, yet seems to call a coach.
The tucked-up semptress walks with hasty strides,
While streams run down her oil'd umbrella's sides.
Here various kinds by various fortunes lead,
Commence acquaintance underneath a shed.
Triumphant Tories and desponding Whigs,
Forget their fewds, and join to save their wigs.
Box'd in a chair the Beau impatient sits,
While spouts run clatt'ring o'er the roof by fits;
And ever and anon with frightful din
The leather sounds, he trembles from within. . . .
Now from all parts the swelling kennels flow,
And bear their trophies with them as they go;
Filth of all hues and odours seem to tell
What street they sail'd from, by their sight and smell.
They, as each torrent drives, with rapid force
From Smithfield, or St Pulchre's shape their course,
And in huge confluent join at Snow-Hill ridge,
Fall from the conduit prone to Holborn Bridge.
Sweepings from butchers' stalls, dung, guts and blood,
Drown'd puppies, stinking sprats, all drench'd in mud,
Dead cats and turnip tops come tumbling down the flood.

JONATHAN SWIFT

★ Swift was proud of this poem and after it had appeared in *The Tatler*
he wrote 'They say 'tis the best thing I ever writ, and I think so too.' (It
was published shortly after the fall of the Whigs when the Tory, Harley,
had come to power.)

LONDON TRAVEL

The Ocean In London

In London while I slowly wake
At morning I'm amazed to hear
The ocean, seventy miles away,
Below my window roaring, near.

When first I know that heavy sound
I keep my eyelids closely down,
And sniff the brine, and hold all thought
Reined back outside the walls of town.

So I can hardly well believe
That those tremendous billows are
Of iron and steel and wood and glass:
Van, lorry, and gigantic car.

HAROLD MONRO (1925)

Strap-Hanging

Now that we are wedged together,
Sweet stranger,
Closer than man and wife,
Why not make the best of this indignity?
Let our blood rioting together,
Murmur stories of our life's adventures,
Just as a river in its course
Brings emblems from its source.

Swing! Swing!
We are shamed, abashed:
Thrown breast to breast.
You dare not look in my eyes
Nor I in yours.

89

And yet in spite of this
I feel strange sympathies
Bearing my heart back
Along some time-tunnelling track
Which I do not recognize
Which I never trod before.

Swing! Swing!
The crowd is wheat
Before the scythe.
You are swept off your feet,
Thrown against me, a wave,
Dashed on a rock.
But we survive the shock.
Could you tell me what you learned!

Could I tell you what I have!
I saw you in the sunshine, a little girl
Sitting on a gate by a farmhouse yard
Eating blackberries out of a handkerchief.

But that must be twenty years ago,
For your face was different then.
Ah!   What a relief,
One or two men
Are getting up to go!
It was not this face

Somewhat pallid with the City.
Time's disgrace
Had not touched it, nor Pity.
But still it was the same.

I do not want to know your name.
We are touching here by chance,
Some experiment of Fate.
Life has barriers, I know.
But was it you upon that gate?
Tell me, tell me ere you go!

But she is gone, without a glance!

RICHARD CHURCH (1928)

A Transport Of Delight
(*The Omnibus*)

Some talk of a Lagonda,
Some like a smart M.G.,
Or for Bonnie Army Lorry
They'd lay them doon and dee.
Such means of locomotion
Seem rather dull to us –
The Driver and Conductor
Of a London Omnibus.

Hold very tight please, ting-ting!

When you are lost in London
And you don't know where you are,
You'll hear my voice a-calling:
'Pass further down the car!'
And very soon you'll find yourself
Inside the Terminus
   In a London Transport
   Diesel-engined
   Ninety-seven horse-power
   Omnibus!

Along the Queen's great highway
I drive my merry load
At twenty miles per hour
In the middle of the road;
We like to drive in convoys –
We're most gregarious;
   The big six-wheeler
   Scarlet-painted
   London Transport
   Diesel-engined
   Ninety-seven horse-power
   Omnibus!

Earth has not anything to show more fair!
Mind the stairs! Mind the stairs!
Earth has not anything to show more fair!
Any more fares? Any more fares?

When cabbies try to pass me,
Before they overtakes,
I sticks me flippin' hand out
As I jams on all me brakes!
Them jackal taxi-drivers
Can only swear and cuss,
    Behind that monarch of the road,
    Observer of the Highway Code,
    That big six-wheeler
    Scarlet-painted
    London Transport
    Diesel-engined
    Ninety-seven horse-power
    Omnibus! . . .

MICHAEL FLANDERS (1952)

Southern Electric

After a week of fog, a mild bright winter morning.
Here I am in the train, reading Wordsworth to work
Without any impatience. Eyes stray from those pastures
And through the window find WANDSWORTH a peaceable
   beast enough,
Sprawling and arching a brick back in the sun.
And look again at the others, no longer lifeless
Waxwork heads nodding, fixed stares at newsprint:
Their eyes are mild with interest, wander without anxiety,
Without any impatience. The pressure is off.
There is no strain in the morning under the blue sky.
Have we ever doubted heaven? Why, already here . . .
At least, until we get to WATERLOO . . .

MARTIN BELL (1967)

Underground

Riding down the moving stairs old fears
of severed feet, a sucked-in doll come back.
Commuters skip lightly off, a daily movement
perfected into an art. I still expect at least
my heel to catch, and stumble off, a beginner
yet again.

Beginning to die is familiar ground for me.
Start all over. You can make it a drama,
accept the worst, face it with dignity,
or say you don't approve, or even do it
yourself without the aid of life machine
or intensive care.

Standing carefully where I am, I trace
the blue Victoria line, remembering the wrong
directions I have taken and all the doors
I should have pushed, but pulled instead,
and all the men like you who took me
for a ride.

Riding still, I sit in my swaying carriage,
and wonder if I'm going North or South.
Am I right for King's Cross, I rehearse
to myself, but everyone seems to know just
where they're at, float to offices on time,
dive and swim.

Swimming through the corridors and past signs
I consider if the bow-wave of multi-coloured
faces are really fish and I am travelling
to be eaten whole, or piecemeal perhaps,
a passing shrimp, part of his daily meal
of fables.

Fabulous rescues like Mrs Bliss who thought
she'd had it off the coast of California,

until a warm snout nudged her to the shallows
place dolphins second only to man, who sport
in schools, but are seldom seen in this
underground oceanarium.

Is it an ocean or a city or a sea-bed?
Let's pretend. Put on your dolphin kit.
Look, it's a secret. Cross my heart
and hope to die, if ever I should tell
a lie. This is a magical kingdom if you have
half an ear or eye.

ELIZABETH BARTLETT (1981)

Thank You!
or
The Muzak-Lovers

Trafalgar Square tube:
Nameless corridors tiled in white
Thick with early tourists on a Sunday in spring.

Coming up at last for air,
My ears catch the strains
Of Pan-like pipes in ecstasy,
And there he stands,
With upward steps to left and right,
Caught in a shaft of soft sunlight,
A shining silver flute at his lips,
A box at his feet,
Lined with a square of richly coloured silk.

As I pause in front of him,
Hand already on my wallet,
I see the box is empty.

I take my time.

94

Open the wallet,
Open the coin purse,
Select some silver,
Listening all the while to the music.
Two tens and two fives
I drop into the box,
Casually as I pass,

And as I do he takes the flute from his mouth.
'Thank *you*!' he says.
I nod, a little shyly,
Lost for words,
Head on up the steps,
As the music starts again.

London Transport's powers that be
Detest live music it seems to me:
With piped Max Bygraves they assail the workers
As they pass harassed through Oxford Circus.

MARK   HAVILAND   (1979)

*A 202**

This coarse road, my road, struggles out
South-east across London, an exhausted
Grey zigzag of stubborn, unassimilable
    Macadam, passing hoardings pasted

With blow-ups of cricket journalists, blackened
And not-quite-Georgian terraces,
Shagged-out Greens of geraniums and
    Floral coats-of-arms, lost pieces

Of genteel façade behind and above
Lyons' shopfronts and 'Pullum Promotions',
– Journeying between wired-off bombed lots glossy
    With parked Consuls, making diversions

Round bus depots and draggled estates
In circumlocutory One-Ways,
Netting aquaria in crammed pet store windows,
    Skirting multi-racial bingo queues,

And acquiring, for its self-hating hoard, old black-railed
Underground bogs advising the Seamen's Hospital,
'Do-it-yourself' shops, 'Funerals and Monuments', and
    Victorian Charrington pubs. All

Along its length it despoils, in turn, a sequence
Of echoless names: Camberwell, Peckham,
New Cross Gate; places having no recorded past
    Except in histories of the tram.

It takes out, in cars, arterial affluence
At week-ends, returning it as bad blood
To Monday mornings in town. It is altogether
    Like a vein travelled by hardy diseases, an aged

Canal dredgeable for bodies left behind
On its soulless travels: Sixty-Nine,
Thirty-Six, One-Eight-Five. It takes no clear
    Attitude anyone could easily define

So as to resist or admire it. It seems to hate you
Possessively, want to envelop you in nothing
Distinguishable or distinguished, like its own
    Smothered slopes and rotting

Valleys. This road, generally, is one for
The long-defeated; and turns any ironic
Observer's tracer-isotope of ecology,
    Sociology, or hopeful manic

Verse into a kind of mere
Nosing virus itself. It leaves its despondent, foul
And intractable deposit on its own
    Banks all the way like virtually all

Large rivers, particularly the holy ones, which it
Is not. It sees little that deserves to be undespised.
It only means well in the worst of ways.
    How much of love is much less compromised?

ALAN BROWNJOHN (1969)

★ This road runs from Vauxhall Bridge through Camberwell and
Peckham to New Cross.

Westminster Abbey

On The Tombs In Westminster Abbey*

Mortality, behold, and fear,
What a change of flesh is here!
Think how many royal bones
Sleep within this heap of stones,
Hence removed from beds of ease,
Dainty fare, and what might please,
Fretted roofs, and costly shows,
To a roof that flats the nose:
Which proclaims all flesh is grass;
How the world's fair glories pass;
That there is no trust in health,
In youth, in age, in greatness, wealth;
For if such could have reprieved
Those had been immortal lived.
Know from this the world's a snare,
How that greatness is but care,
How all pleasures are but pain,
And how short they do remain:
For here they lie had realms and lands,
That now want strength to stir their hands;
Where from their pulpits sealed with dust
They preach: 'In greatness is no trust'.
Here's an acre sown indeed
With the richest royal seed,
That the earth did e'er suck in
Since the first man died for sin . . .
Here's a world of pomp and state,
Forgotten dead, disconsolate;
Think, then, this scythe that mows down kings
Exempts no meaner mortal things. . . .

FRANCIS BEAUMONT (1603)

* Beaumont himself is buried in Westminster Abbey close to Chaucer and Spencer.

An Address To The Very Reverend John Ireland, D.D.

The Dean And Chapter of Westminster

Oh, very reverend Dean and Chapter,
  Exhibitors of giant men,
Hail to each surplice-backed Adapter
  Of England's dead, in her Stone den!
Ye teach us properly to prize
  Two-shilling Grays, and Gays, and Handels,
And, to throw light upon our eyes
  Deal in Wax Queens like old wax candles. . . .

The profitable Abbey is
  A sacred 'Change for stony stock,
Not that a speculation 'tis –
  The profit's founded on a rock.
Death, Dean, and Doctors, in each nave
  Bony investments have inurned!
And hard 'twould be to find a grave
  From which 'no money is returned!' . . .

Oh, licensed cannibals, ye eat
  Your dinners from your own dead race,
Think Gray, preserved, a 'funeral meat',
  And Dryden, deviled, after grace,
A relish; – and you take your meal
  From Rare Ben Jonson underdone,
Or, whet your holy knives on Steele,
  To cut away at Addison! . . .

Put up in Poet's Corner, near
  The little door, a platform small;
Get there a monkey – never fear,
  You'll catch the gapers one and all!

104

Stand each of ye a Body Guard,
    A Trumpet under either fin,
And yell away in Palace Yard
    'All dead! All dead! Walk in! Walk in!' . . .

THOMAS HOOD (1820)

★ This spirited attack did lead to the Dean reducing the entrance charge
from two shillings. The controversy as to whether places of worship
should charge tourists continues. There was a lengthy and impassioned
correspondence in *The Times* in 1980 on exactly this issue. The current
position is that the main body of the Abbey is free to all but there is a
charge to see the royal chapels – fifty pence (or ten shillings).

In Westminster Abbey

Let me take this other glove off
    As the *vox humana* swells,
And the beauteous fields of Eden
    Bask beneath the Abbey bells.
Here, where England's statesmen lie,
Listen to a lady's cry.

Gracious Lord, oh bomb the Germans.
    Spare their women for Thy Sake.
And if that is not too easy
    We will pardon Thy Mistake.
But, gracious Lord, whate'er shall be,
Don't let anyone bomb me.

Keep our Empire undismembered
    Guide our Forces by Thy Hand,
Gallant blacks from far Jamaica,
    Honduras and Togoland;
Protect them Lord in all their fights,
And, even more, protect the whites.

Think of what our Nation stands for,
    Books from Boots' and country lanes,
Free speech, free passes, class distinction,
    Democracy and proper drains.

Lord, put beneath Thy special care
One-eighty-nine Cadogan Square.

Although dear Lord I am a sinner,
   I have done no major crime;
Now I'll come to Evening Service
   Whensoever I have the time.
So, Lord, reserve for me a crown,
And do not let my shares go down.

I will labour for Thy Kingdom,
   Help our lads to win the war,
Send white feathers to the cowards
   Join the Women's Army Corps,
Then wash the Steps around Thy Throne
In the Eternal Safety Zone.

Now I feel a little better,
   What a treat to hear Thy Word,
Where the bones of leading statesmen,
   Have so often been interr'd.
And now, dear Lord, I cannot wait
Because I have a luncheon date.

JOHN BETJEMAN (1940)

To The Statues In Poets' Corner, Westminster Abbey

You stony bunch of pockskinned whiteys,
Why kip in here? Who sentenced you?
They are buying postcards of you,
The girls in safety knickers.
Tombfaces, glumbums,
Wine should be jumping out of all your holes,
You should have eyes that roll, arms that knock things
   over,
Legs that falter and working cocks.
Listen.

On William Blake's birthday we're going to free you,
Blast you off your platforms with a blowtorch full of
    brandy
And then we'll all stomp over to the Houses of Parliament
And drive them into the Thames with our bananas.

ADRIAN MITCHELL (1968)

Do Not Go Sober*

Do not go sober into that dim light.
Young bards should burp and belch at end of day;
Rage, rage against that crabby, Abbey site.

Though poets at their end know wrong is right
Because their words have left them legless they
Do not go sober into that dim light.

Good men, who know what sweat it is to write,
And cheat and sponge and get their end away
Rage, rage against that crabby, Abbey site.

Wild men who did their best when they were tight
And languished when they kept the booze at bay
Do not go sober into that dim light.

Grave men, now dead, who know, as well they might,
Memorial plaques diminish human clay,
Rage, rage against that crabby, Abbey site.

And you, Lord Byron, lying on my right,
Proving that dissolution rules OK,
Do not go sober into that dim light.
Rage, rage against that crabby, Abbey site.

ROGER WOODDIS (1981)

* This was Roger Woddis's comment in *Punch* on the news that, follow-ing a remark made by the former U.S. President, Jimmy Carter, as he was being shown around Westminster Abbey, Dylan Thomas is now to have a niche in Poets' Corner. This parody is based upon Thomas's famous poem 'Do not go gentle into that good night'.

The West: Kensington to Kew

Kensington Gardens[*]
The Tramps

The tramps slink in at half past four
in the sweet summer weather,
and stretch upon the grass and snore
peaceably all together.

They look like litter on the grass,
(and not like sleeping men)
that life - the feaster - dropped, and has
not tidied up again.

HUMBERT WOLFE (c 1930)

[*] Several kings lived in Kensington Palace but the Gardens were the resort of layabouts and petty criminals. In them George II was waylaid by a highwayman and deprived of his purse, his watch and his buckles.

In Sloane Square

May she not think, the naked bronze
Suspended in the autumn air
Without a thought are fallen leaves
And women blown about the square?

Her solid metal, quietly,
Reposes in a single thought
They clutch their skirts, and squint at her
As miscellaneously distraught.

Not one leaf falls to hide her shame
And they are muffled cosily
Yet the veiled tenderness is hers
And theirs the brazen nudity.

C. H. SISSON (1959)

111

Paddington Canal

A mocking mirror, the black water turns
Tall houses upside down, makes learned men
Walk on their heads in squares of burning light;
Lovers like folded bats hang in a kiss,
Swaying as if a breeze could sever them.
The barges, giant sea-birds fast asleep,
Lie on the surface, moored and motionless;
Then, drowning gently, are drawn down to join
The sunken lovers and the acrobats.
Out of the grim dimensions of a street
Slowly I see another landscape grow
Downwards into a lost reality;
A magic mirror, the black water tells
Of a reversed Atlantis wisely built
To catch and to transform
The wasted substance of our daily acts,
Accommodate our mad and lovely doubles
In a more graceful city timelessly.

MICHAEL HAMBURGER (1949)

Lament For
'The Old Swan',
Notting Hill Gate

The Old Swan has gone. They have widened the road.
A year ago they closed her, and she stood,
The neighbouring houses pulled down, suddenly revealed
In all her touching pretentiousness
Of turret and Gothic pinnacle, like
A stupid and ugly woman
Unexpectedly struck to dignity by bereavement.

112

And now she has vanished. The gap elicits
A guarded sentiment. Enough bad poets
Have romanticized beer and pubs,
And those for whom the gimcrack enchantments
Of engraved glass, mahogany, plants in pots,
Were all laid out to please, are fugitives, doubtless,
Nightly self-immersed in a fake splendour.

Yet a Public House perhaps makes manifest also
The hidden City; implies its laws
Of tolerance, hierarchy, exchange.
Friends I remember there, enemies, acquaintances,
Some drabs and drunks, some bores and boors, and many
Indifferent and decent people. They will drink elsewhere.
Anonymous, it harboured
The dreadful, innocent martyrs
Of megalopolis – Christie or Heath.

Now that's finished with. And all the wide
And sober roads of the world walk sensibly onwards
Into the featureless future. But the white swans
That dipped and swam in each great lucid mirror
Remain in the mind only, remain as a lost symbol.

JOHN HEATH-STUBBS (1950)

Earls Court

Earls Court – a bourgeois slum,
Well the wrong side of that dividing line
That runs down west of Knightsbridge, north to south,
Invisible but strong to separate
All those with Capital from those without.

This is the country of the single room,
The two-room flat, three single girls who share.
The secretaries who have families
In the Home Counties. (Young executives
Exhaust their nights with noisy male displays
Of potency in tiger-roaring cars.)

113

Home perms and frozen food.
Nail-varnished stockings where the ladders are!

And students. Indians and Africans, the sons of chiefs,
Intelligent and well-behaved and far
Removed from Notting Hill's black heart
Where the poor whites would carve you for a giggle –
Though just a mile north as the jim crow flies.

Australians too. In groups in Earls Court Road,
In solidarity that will not move for prams,
Like little clots in the pedestrian bloodstream
That flows along the pavements.

Sweaters and jeans. Some beards. For in Earls Court
Live bachelors (boys and girls),
The adolescents and the very old.
The families with children – very few.

The old, like refugees,
Into the hotels of the Cromwell Road
Have all retired. To leave the world behind,
With TV, knitting, books and cups of tea.

And what has Earls Court got? A Hall
For Exhibitions; and the Empress Hall
(For boxing, Louis Armstrong, and the rest);
New, high and mighty, looms
The Empress State Building – from Holland Park
A summer's landmark.
A Station (District and Piccadilly Lines)
Known to commuters as a terminal.
Victorian streets and squares
Like living memories
Of that Great Exhibition (1851).
Hotels for oldies. Restaurants a few.
Churches. Some coffee bars for student life.
Some hospitals (my son was born in one).
Some shops, some pubs. Nothing spectacular.

What Earls Court has is this:
A sense of free and easy. There are no Joneses
For anybody to keep up with here.
The negroes in the snow are beautiful,
And you can wear what clothes you damn well please.
No debs. No escorts. No tycoons. But life
In great variety. Eccentrics, too,
Who in a bus will tell the passengers:
'To-day's the Birthday of The Princess Royal.
I'm telling you because you ought to know.'
A lady neat, precise, a bit insane.

Yes, that's the nut-shell truth. Earls Court
Was never smart. Nor likely, much, to be.

GAVIN EWART (1964)

Turnham Green*

All the angels at Turnham Green
Survey a gentle, idyllic scene –
Wide-winged, blue-eyed, English ones,
With their hair tied up in buns.
How lucidly they look – behold
Privet hedges green and gold
Round tiny gardens prettified
With stocks and pinks and London Pride,
Of houses built on a modest plan,
Semi-detached Victorian,
With freshly painted doors that shine
All along the District Line.
By Supermarket and Odeon
Celestial guardians march on.

These Angels do not weep; they sigh
When the fireside Cyclops opens its eye;
And I suspect they are not fond
Of the Bingo club and the Premium Bond.
Softly secure the lambs are sleeping,
Each within the angelic keeping.

115

I met one face I seemed to know –
The ghost of Ugo Foscolo;
He said: 'The year that Byron shook
The dust of England off I took
The devious path the exile knows.
I left the Ionian isle where blows
Salt-tanged from off Homeric seas
The wind between the Olive-trees.
Fresh were my hopes and tall my pride –
The doors of Holland House stood wide –
But still my path went winding down,
To Soho first then Camden Town.
At St Johns Wood I lived and sang,
With oranges and lemons to hang

On boughs of English trees, in vain –
Zante would not come back again.
Seek not my grave to waste a tear –
Was ever Poet easy here?
Translated now my bones; they lie
Where Arno, not sad Thames, runs by.'

He vanished, as a steel guitar
Tinkled out of a coffee-bar:
The little lambs of Turnham Green
Were in their pasture here, between
The Apocalypse and Eden's ground,
Out of shot of the Trumpet's sound.

JOHN HEATH-STUBBS (1968)

★ Foscolo was the celebrated Italian poet who praised the French Revo-
lution and Napoleon but he died in exile and poverty in Turnham Green
in 1827. He wrote only sixteen poems but they are regarded as master-
pieces in Italian literature.

Go Down To Kew In Lilac Time

Go down to Kew in lilac-time, in lilac-time, in lilac-time.
  Go down to Kew in lilac-time (it isn't far from
    London!),

And you shall wander hand in hand with love in summer's
    wonderland.
    Go down to Kew in lilac-time (it isn't far from
      London!).

The cherry-trees are seas of bloom and soft perfume and
    sweet perfume,
    The cherry-trees are seas of bloom (and oh, so near to
      London!),
And there they say when dawn is high and all the world's a
    blaze of sky,
    The cuckoo, though he's very shy, will sing a song for
      London.

The Dorian nightingale is rare, and yet they say you'll hear
    him there
    At Kew, at Kew in lilac-time (and oh, so near to
      London!),
The linnet and the throstle, too, and after dark the long
    halloo
    And golden-eyed *tu-whit, tu-whoo,* of owls that ogle
      London.

For Noah hardly knew a bird of any kind that isn't heard
    At Kew, at Kew in lilac-time (and oh, so near to
      London!),
And when the rose begins to pout and all the chestnut
    spires are out
    You'll hear the rest without a doubt, all chorussing for
      London:

Come down to Kew in lilac-time, in lilac-time, in lilac-time;
    Come down to Kew in lilac-time (it isn't far from London!),
And you shall wander hand in hand with love in summer's
    wonderland;
    Come down to Kew in lilac-time (it isn't far from London!).

ALFRED NOYES (c. 1910)
from *The Barrel-Organ*

The East End and Hackney

If It Wasn't For The 'Ouses In Between*

If you saw my little backyard, 'Wot a pretty spot!' you'd
    cry,
It's a picture on a sunny summer day;
Wiv the turnip tops and cabbages wot peoples doesn't buy
I makes it on a Sunday look all gay.
The neighbours finks I grow 'em and you'd fancy you're in
    Kent,
Or at Epsom if you gaze into the mews.
It's a wonder as the landlord doesn't want to raise the rent,
Because we've got such nobby distant views.

Oh it really is a wery pretty garden
And Chingford to the eastward could be seen;
Wiv a ladder and some glasses,
You could see to 'Ackney Marshes,
If it wasn't for the 'ouses in between. . . .

We're as countrified as can be wiv a clothes prop for a tree,
The tub-stool makes a rustic little stile;
Ev'ry time the bloomin' clock strikes there's a cuckoo sings
    to me,
And I've painted up 'To Leather Lane a mile.'
Wiv tomatoes and wiv radishes wot 'adn't any sale,
The backyard looks a puffick mass o' bloom;
And I've made a little beehive wiv some beetles in a pail,
And a pitchfork wiv a handle of a broom.

Oh it really is a wery pretty garden,
And Rye 'ouse from the cock-loft could be seen:
Where the chickweed man undresses,
To bathe 'mong the watercresses,
If it wasn't for the 'ouses in between.

EDGAR BATEMAN (c. 1900)

* This was sung by Gus Elen.

In Limehouse*

In Limehouse, in Limehouse, before the break of day,
I hear the feet of many men who go upon their way,
Who wander through the City.
The grey and cruel City.
Through streets that have no pity,
The streets where men decay.

In Limehouse, in Limehouse, by night as well as day,
I hear the feet of children who go to work or play,
Of children born to sorrow,
The workers of tomorrow,
How shall they work tomorrow
Who get no bread today.

In Limehouse, in Limehouse, today and every day
I see the weary mothers who sweat their souls away:
Poor, tired mothers, trying
To hush the feeble crying
Of little babies dying
For want of bread today.

In Limehouse, in Limehouse, I'm dreaming of the day
When evil time shall perish and be driven clean away,
When father, child and mother
Shall live and love each other,
And brother help his brother
In happy work and play.

CLEMENT ATTLEE (c. 1921)

* In 1918 Major Clement Attlee went into local politics in the East End
and became the first Labour Mayor of Stepney. In 1922 he was elected
to represent Limehouse. This poem was published by the *Socialist Review*
whose editor was a gangling Scot, Ramsay MacDonald. In 1924 Attlee
got his first foot on the ladder which was to lead him to Number 10, as
the Parliamentary Private Secretary to the first Labour Prime Minister
– MacDonald.

October 1936*

We stood at Gardiner's Corner,
We stood and watched the crowds,
We stood at Gardiner's Corner,
Firm, solid, voices loud.

Came the marching of the blackshirts,
Came the pounding of their feet,
Came the sound of ruffians marching
Where the five roads meet.

We thought of many refugees
Fleeing from the fascist hordes,
The maimed, the sick,
The young, the old,
Those who had fought the fascist lords.

So we stopped them there at Gardiner's,
We fought and won our way.
We fought the baton charges,
No fascist passed that day!

MILLY HARRIS (1971)

---

* About 3000 black-shirted fascists, led by Mosley, planned to march
through the East End on 4 October 1936. The residents, rallied by Jewish
and Communist groups, literally filled the roads at Gardiner's Corner
and Cable Street to stop the march. Over one hundred thousand people
were said to be in the streets and some 7000 police tried to keep order.
Mosley, after a consultation with the Commissioner of Police, thought
better and marched his men westwards down the Embankment. The
jubilant crowds cheered. They did not pass.

Whitechapel in Britain

Pumbedita, Cordova, Cracow, Amsterdam,
Vilna, Lublin, Berditchev and Volozhin,
Your names will always be sacred,
Places where Jews have been.

And sacred is Whitechapel,
It is numbered with our Jewish towns.
Holy, holy, holy
Are your bombed stones.

If we ever have to leave Whitechapel,
As other Jewish towns were left,
Its soul will remain a part of us,
Woven into us, woof and weft.

AVRAM STENCL (c. 1940)

Hackney

Why is Hackney called 'Hackney'?
Why could it not be 'Dirty'?
Its name stinks of steam and smoke.
How much longer do I have to live in this place?
Everybody wants to leave and try to forget about Hackney.

But I can't:
It's groaning inside me
And that is why everybody smokes
To forget about it.
Everybody wants to leave and go to the country.

VIVIAN USHERWOOD (1972)

Saturday Morning In Angel Lane

Down the Lane on a Saturday morning,
When the place is on the go,
Stalls are open and the grafters working,
Alf and Eddie and May and Flo.

O, you noisy city,
O, you sprawling city,
O, you're my old city.

Women pass with their hair in curlers,
Lads stroll by with hair unshorn,
And the girls on five-inch heels go tripping,
Known 'em all since they were born.

O, you noisy city,
O, you sprawling city,
O, you're my old city.

As you walk on a Saturday morning,
Past the fruit and winkle stands
Get the tangy sea smell for a moment
And the breath of distant lands.

O, you noisy city,
O, you sprawling city,
O, you're my old city.

Down the Lane on a Saturday morning,
Underneath the London sky,
With the city borne upon their shoulders,
Men and women go walking by.

O, you noisy city,
O, you sprawling city,
O, you're my old city.

EWAN MacCOLL (1978)

Stepney

I think Stepney is a very smokey place
But I like it
People in Stepney do things wrong
But I like them
Everything in Stepney has its disadvantages
But I like it.

It does not have clean air like the country
But I like it
The buildings are old and cold
But I like them
The summer is not very hot
But I like it.

ROSEMARIE DALE (1973)

Stoke Newington Churchyard

On a bend in the road by the old town hall
a country churchyard survives
where the villagers of two hundred years ago
sleep under our present-day lives.

The ancient ravaged stones still speak
of times etched sharp by loss.
Today is a drug-numbed, dream-smudged place;
who are the shades, them or us?

Their span was short, yet they still endure
as epitaphs of village history:
'Here lie the remains of Elizabeth Ann Love
who departed this life in her infancy.'

And while the freighters thunder past
raising a dusty pall,
Emmanuel William Pickett fades,
'slain by pirates in the Bay of Bengal'.

SHONA BURNS (1981)

The Thames

A Waterman's Litany

Come slithe with me and be my love
And we will all the Boroughs gove
in
Darkhouse Lane
Stew Lane
Cousin Lane
Pudding Lane
Gardeners Lane
Fye Foot Lane
Wig Lane
Duck Foot's Lane
Bull Wharf Lane
Mincing Lane
on
Garlick Hill
Old Fish Street Hill
Bread Street Hill
Huggin Hill
Dowgate Hill
by
Broken Wharf
Sunlight Wharf
Puddle Dock
Vitrea Wharf
Paul's Pier Wharf
Crown and Horseshoe Wharf
Abbey Wharf
Red Bull Wharf
or over in the Savage Gardens
or down to the Prospect of Whitby
If nomenclature may you move
Then slithe with me and be my love.

EUGENE WALTER (1955)
from *The Shapes of the River*

Upon Westminster Bridge[*]

Earth has not anything to show more fair:
Dull would he be of soul who could pass by
A sight so touching in its majesty:
This City now doth like a garment wear

The beauty of the morning: silent, bare,
Ships, towers, domes, theatres, and temples lie
Open unto the fields, and to the sky,
All bright and glittering in the smokeless air.

Never did sun more beautifully steep
In his first splendour valley, rock, or hill;
Ne'er saw I, never felt, a calm so deep!

The river glideth at his own sweet will:
Dear God! the very houses seem asleep;
And all that mighty heart is lying still!

WILLIAM WORDSWORTH (3 September 1802)

* Westminster Bridge was the second bridge to be built after London
Bridge and was completed in 1750 at a cost of £400,000. Boswell, rather
more earthy than Wordsworth, recorded that he picked up a girl in the
Haymarket and took her to Westminster Bridge as he wanted to make
love to her on that 'noble edifice'.

Dockland[*]

Cranes standing still, no work for them
No movement, a monument to times past.
Silhouette outlined against a London sky.

Their reflection, mirrored in the waters
of a silent dock.
Casting their shadows across the decks
of pleasure yachts.

Like a cancer spreading, with unchecked speed,
Wharves, warehouses closed overnight

132

Transformed, renovated
Not for people who have no place to live,
But for those who with obscene ease,
Sail their yachts whenever they please,
Leaving them moored outside their second homes.
It's all a part of our social disease.

Docks closed,
Once where dock workers played their part,
Shifting cargo, keeping London alive.
Now silence reigns, it is supreme,
Thrusting aside this industrial scene.

Gone now, this way of life,
Testimony to the power of those few,
Whose decisions carry far and wide,
Eroding, encroaching, changing the
Character of our riverside.

BERNIE STEER (1975)

★ Bernie Steer was one of the four East End dockers who were imprisoned
in 1972 as a result of their opposition to the Conservative Government's
reform of industrial relations. They were dramatically released by the
intervention of the Official Solicitor. In his lament for the death of the
London Docks he overlooks the contribution which the restrictive prac-
tices of the dockers made. The modern upper docks had a life of about
one hundred years. The Royal Victoria Dock was built in 1855, Millwall
Dock in 1868 and the Royal Albert Dock in 1880. Now they are all
closed.

The Distant Prospect

A mighty mass of brick, and smoke, and shipping,
   Dirty and dusky, but as wide as eye
Could reach, with here and there a sail just skipping
   In sight, then lost amidst the forestry
Of masts; wilderness of steeples peeping
   On tiptoe through their sea-coal canopy;
A huge, dun Cupola, like a foolscap crown
On a fool's head – and there is London Town!

LORD BYRON (1823)

Paddle Steamers Near Charing Cross

Well-known as Shilling Sicks, they rolled
Round from Shanklin to Potters Bar . . .
Well, they take a lot of stopping
Do floating volcanoes awash
With beer and dogends.
                Big bottomed
As jolly women they brazened
Off to Dunkirk once in a calm
Summer, came back loaded to their
Dirty funnel-tops with squaddies
Singing Sod The War and turning
Their backs on it, but not for long.

Now it's the full cosmetic job,
Not a barnacle, french letter,
Or rusty rifle to be seen,
History's slung over the blunt end
Where it belongs; this one's a pub
A wot-we-want-is-wotneys place
At £10 a pint, the other
A Gallery, rather chic, not
A rude postcard in sight, and the
Only frilly Knicker leg
The one Elizabeth the first
Has round her neck.
              Ghosts? They shoved off
Like history, over the blunt end
Into the tide no paddles thrash,
Gone where the straw man goes, my son,
Like the Dodo.

GERRY WELLS (1981)

134

Embankment At Night,
Before The War

Outcasts

. . . At Charing Cross, here, beneath the bridge
Sleep in a row the outcasts,
Packed in a line with their heads against the wall.
Their feet in a broken ridge
Stretched out on the way, and a lout casts
A look as he stands on the edge of this naked stall.

Beasts that sleep will cover
Their face in their flank; so these
Have huddled rags or limbs on the naked sleep.
Save, as the tram-cars hover
Past with the noise of a breeze
And gleam as of sunshine crossing the low black heap,

Two naked faces are seen
Bare and asleep,
Two pale clots swept by the light of the cars.

Foam-clots showing between
The long, low tidal-heap,
The mud-weed opening two pale, shadowless stars.

Over the pallor of only two faces
Passes the gallivant beam of the trams;
Shows in only two sad places
The white bare bone of our shams.

A little, bearded man, peaked in sleeping,
With a face like a chickweed flower.
And a heavy woman, sleeping still keeping
Callous and dour.

Over the pallor of only two places
Tossed on the low, black, ruffled heap
Passes the light of the tram as it races
Out of the deep. . . .

On the outer pavement, slowly,
Theatre people pass,
Holding aloft their umbrellas that flash and are bright
Like flowers of infernal moly
Over nocturnal grass
Wetly bobbing and drifting away on our sight.

And still by the rotten row of shattered feet,
Outcasts keep guard.
Forgotten,
Forgetting, till fate shall delete
One from the ward.

The factories on the Surrey side
Are beautifully laid in black on a gold-grey sky.
The river's invisible tide
Threads and thrills like ore that is wealth to the eye.

And great gold midges
Cross the chasm
At the bridges
Above intertwined plasm.

D. H. LAWRENCE (c. 1930)

Rising Damp*

A river can sometimes be diverted, but it is a very hard thing to lose it altogether. (J. G. Head: paper read to the Auctioneers' Institute, 1907.)

At our feet they lie low,
The little fervent underground
Rivers of London

(Effra, Graveney, Falcon, Quaggy,
Wandle, Walbrook, Tyburn, Fleet)

Whose names are disfigured,
Frayed, effaced.

These are the Magogs that chewed the clay
To the basin that London nestles in.
These are the currents that chiselled the city,
That washed the clothes and turned the mills,
Where children drank and salmon swam
And wells were holy.

They have gone under.
Boxed, like the magician's assistant.
Buried alive in earth.
Forgotten, like the dead.

They return spectrally after heavy rain,
Confounding suburban gardens. They infiltrate
Chronic bronchitis statistics. A silken
Slur haunts dwellings by shrouded
Watercourses, and is taken
For the footing of the dead.

Being of our world, they will return
(Westbourne, caged at Sloane Square,
Will jack from his box),

Will deluge cellars, detonate manholes,
Plant effluent on our faces,
Sink the city

(Effra, Graveney, Falcon, Quaggy,
Wandle, Walbrook, Tyburn, Fleet)

It is the other rivers that lie
Lower, that touch us only in dreams
That never surface. We feel their tug
As a dowser's rod bends to the source below

(Phlegethon, Acheron, Lethe, Styx).

U. A. FANTHORPE (1981)

★ The little rivers of London which flow into the Thames were used as
sewers and rubbish tips, and have been progressively covered over. In
1766 a drunken butcher fell into the Fleet where, entrapped in the mud,
he froze to death; which persuaded the City fathers to convert the Fleet
from an open sewer to a closed one.

Sweet Thames Flow Softly

I met my girl at Woolwich Pier, beneath a big crane
    standing,
And, Oh, the love I felt for her it passed all understanding.
    Took her sailing on the river,
      flow, sweet river, flow,
    London Town was mine to give her,
      sweet Thames flow softly.
    Made the Thames into a crown,
      flow, sweet river, flow,
    Made a brooch of Silvertown,
      sweet Thames flow softly.

At London Yard I held her hand, at Blackwall Point I faced
    her,
At the Isle of Dogs I kissed her mouth and tenderly
    embraced her.
        Heard the bells of Greenwich ringing,
           flow, sweet river, flow,
        All the time my heart was singing,
           sweet Thames flow softly.
        Limehouse Reach I gave her there,
           flow, sweet river, flow,
        As a ribbon for her hair,
           sweet Thames flow softly.

From Shadwell Dock to Nine Elms Reach we cheek to
    cheek were dancing,
Her necklace, made of London Bridge, her beauty was
    enhancing.
        Kissed her once again at Wapping,
           flow, sweet river, flow,
        After that there was no stopping,
           sweet Thames flow softly.
        Richmond Park it was her ring,
           flow, sweet river, flow,
        I'd have given her anything,
           sweet Thames flow softly.

From Rotherhithe to Putney Bridge my love I was
    declaring,
And she, from Kew to Isleworth, her love to me was
    swearing.
        Love had set my heart a-burning,
           flow, sweet river, flow,
        Never saw the tide was turning,
           sweet Thames flow softly.
        Gave her Hampton Court to twist,
           flow, sweet river, flow,
        Into a bracelet for her wrist,
           sweet Thames flow softly.

Now, alas, the tide has changed, my love she has gone from
 me,
And winter's frost has touched my heart and put a blight
 upon me.
     Creeping fog is on the river,
      flow, sweet river, flow,
     Sun and moon and stars gone with her,
      sweet Thames flow softly.
     Swift the Thames runs to the sea,
      flow, sweet river, flow,
     Bearing ships and part of me,
      sweet Thames flow softly.

           EWAN MacCOLL (1979)

South London

Battersea 1948*

to Henry Moore

Three chimneys soar against a violet haze,
A coil of smoke about each towering rim
Writhing and red caught in the sun's last rays,
The distant descant in this modern hymn
To harnessed power, served by its hidden team,
That governs indifferently the nights and days.

Three sculptured forms among the pillared trees,
Timelessly anxious in their prison of stone,
The heavy drapery about their knees
Echoing the burden kindred to each one
That each within herself must bear alone,
Since the uptilted heads spy no release.

W. J. STRACHAN (1950)

* Battersea Power Station, which had a fourth chimney added, has now
been taken out of commission. It will be preserved since it is too costly
to demolish and there are many who want to keep it as a magnificent
memorial to a past industrial age. The Henry Moore statues, which the
sculptor gave himself, can be found on a little mound in the Park close
to the Power Station.

Vauxhall

Pulling through cliffs of windows
We stop at the platform:
Murky, misty; damp haloes round the lights—
The graffiti half lost in dust.

The train gives an orgasmic shudder
And falls silent.
The few passengers gaze vacantly about.
One gives a racking sigh.

Vauxhall. The word blooms in my mind,
Opening up green vistas. Down one of them
My mother, playing the piano,
Waiting for her washing to dry, and singing tremulously:

> *When Lady Betty passes by*
> *I strive to catch her bright blue eye*
> *At Vauxhall in the morning.*

Round her elbow I can just make out the words.
Her hands are crinkly from the soapsuds;
Outside, the roses catch at the blown sheets,
And in Vauxhall, it is all blossom and glances.

I smile out at the grimy wall
(*Wogs sod off—Arsenal are shit*)
And the train throbs back to life,
Sliding us on to some more ordinary place.

CONNIE BENSLEY (1981)

Brixton

You can keep the newspapers:
Nothing happens for us, here.
Even the soot is old, old,
And the weeds in the cracks of our back yards
Have strayed from counties we cannot imagine.
Our windows are curtained, blind.

That old man in the white terrace
Remembers a village, downs.
We remember nothing, here.

Why the black looks, neighbour:
But for us your white would be grayer.
In the park your children and ours
Kick dead leaves for conkers.

MICHAEL HAMBURGER (1968)

The Imperial War Museum

Before us, a morning
of emblems and memories
A squirrel sat on the lawn
like a sketchy fleur-de-lys
on a tattered flag
and trembled as it fed –
a prey to shell-shock
from the autumn bombardment.
Goose-stepping pigeons
pecked about the paving-stones,
where orts of reminiscence
fell from our table,
with its empty tent of toast,
gun-turret of black coffee.

CHRISTOPHER REID (1979)

High Rise In Peckham

High rise flats, towering blocks,
11 – 12 – 14 floors, and more.
Reaching well into the sky
Modern times, people live,
But – is it living?
Cut off from the friendly chat,
Going up into the lift, open the door,
That's that –
High rise flats – the crazy design,
The isolation that becomes a living hell.
Trapped like an animal in a cell.
No contact – oh yes! it's ultra-modern,
But – the loneliness – the high rise flats.
They call it architectural design
Living despair – but of course,
This – is modern times.

P.B. (1980)

145

Catford 1933

The light creaks
    and escalates to rusty dawn
The iron stove ignites the freezing room.
Last night's dinner cast off
    popples in the embers.
My mother lives in a steaming sink.
Boiled haddock condenses on my plate
    Its body cries for the sea.
My father is shouldering his braces like a rifle,
    and brushes the crumbling surface of his suit.
The *Daily Herald* lays jaundiced on the table.
'Jimmy Maxton speaks in Hyde Park',
My father places his unemployment cards
    in his wallet – there's plenty of room for them.
In greaseproof paper, my mother wraps my
        banana sandwiches.
It's 5.40. Ten minutes to catch that
        last workman train.
Who's the last workman? Is it me? I might be famous.
My father and I walk out and are eaten by
        yellow freezing fog.
Somewhere, the Prince of Wales
        and Mrs Simpson are having
        morning tea in bed.
God Save the King.
But God help the rest of us.

SPIKE MILLIGAN (1979)

Snow In Bromley

As of some unproved right, the snow
Settles the outer suburbs now,
Laying its claim unhurriedly
On gnome and monkey-puzzle-tree.

Observe its power to shape and build,
Even in this unfruitful world,
Its white informal fantasies,
From roofs and paths and rockeries.

And swayed by such soft moods, I fall
Into forgiving nearly all
The aspirations of the place,
And what it does to save its face:

The calm and dutiful obsession
With what is 'best in our position',
The loyal and realistic views,
The rush-hours with the *Evening News* –

The snow fulfils its pure design
And softens every ugly line,
And for a while will exorcize
These virulent proprieties.

Within one mile of here there is
No lovelier place to walk than this,
On days when these kind flakes decide
That what it boasts of, they shall hide.

ALAN BROWNJOHN (1961)

From Too Close

at the Royal Greenwich Observatory
the gatekeeper
asked us for
the time

NYKI BLATCHLEY (1980)

Knock'd 'em in the Old Kent Road

Last week down our alley comes a toff,
Nice old geezer with a nasty cough,
Sees my Missus, takes 'is topper off
   In a very gentlemanly way!
'Ma'am', says he, 'I'ave some news to tell,
Your rich Uncle Tom of Camberwell,
Popped off recent, which it ain't a sell,
   Leaving you 'is little Donkey Shay.'

  'Wot cher!' all the neighbours cried,
  'Who're yer goin' to meet Bill?
  Have yer bought the street Bill?'
  Laugh! I thought I should 'ave died,
  Knock'd 'em in the Old Kent Road! . . .

ALBERT CHEVALIER (1890)

Dear, Damn'd Distracting Town, Farewell!

A Farewell To London, In The Year 1715

Dear, damn'd distracting town, farewell!
  Thy fools no more I'll tease:
This year in peace, ye critics, dwell,
  Ye harlots, sleep at ease!

Why should I stay? Both parties rage;
  My vixen mistress squalls;
The wits in envious feuds engage;
  And Homer (damn him!) calls.

Why make I friendships with the great,
  When I no favour seek?
Or follow girls seven hours in eight?
  I need but once a week.

Luxurious lobster-nights, farewell,
  For sober studious days!
And Burlington's delicious meal,
  For salads, tarts and pease!

Adieu to all but Gay alone,
  Whose soul, sincere and free,
Loves all mankind, but flatters none,
  And so may starve with me.

ALEXANDER POPE

Down And Out In London

In London I didn't see the Beatles.
In London I didn't see the Stones.
In London I didn't see Peter Sellers telling mod
    kinky stories to Princess Margaret and
    Anthony Armstrong-Jones
While internationally famous hairdressers
And internationally skinny models
Did corrupt but trendy things to each other
At private clubs.

In London I saw Museums and Towers.
In London I saw them change the guard.
In London I ate a lot of meat pies with one piece
    of meat blended with three pounds of lard,
Followed by a walk in the rain
And another one of those afternoon teas
With the shredded lettuce leaves
On tissue paper.

In London I'd planned to change my image.
In London I haven't changed a thing.
In London I'm standing on the King's Road
With wet feet,
Indigestion,
The wrong hemline,
A run in my pantyhose,
The Oxford Book of English Verse,
And a continuing inability to swing
Even in London.

JUDITH VIORST (1972)

On The Way Home

Like questing hounds
The lechers run through London
From all the alley-ways
Into all the thoroughfares

Until, shoulder to shoulder, they vanish
Into the main line stations
Or the Underground traps them.

A moment of promiscuity at nightfall
Their feet go homewards but their attentions
Are on the nape of a neck or the cut of a thigh
Almost any woman
As Schopenhauer noted
Being more interesting to them than those
Who made their beds that morning.

C. H. SISSON (1950)

Maybe It's Because . . . *

Oh, how I miss you, London fair,
The centre-piece of all my dreaming,
With friendly pimps in Leicester Square
And cut-price dope and coppers beaming.
The streets I used to know,
Where dogs were wont to go,
And I could hear the city's gentle sounds,
Or buy a girl with whips,
A meal of fish and chips,
And still have tenpence change from fifty pounds!

I still recall the spotless trains,
The ticket Jimmy Savile sold one,
That brought me here to Milton Keynes,
A new town drabber than the old one.
I see the hot-dog stands,
The cowboy's well-washed hands,
The ice-cream seller smiling like a shark;
But most of all, through tears,
Among my souvenirs –
The shy apprentice muggers in the park!

ROGER WODDIS (1981)

★ This *Punch* piece was provoked by the announcement that the 1981
Census showed a sizeable exodus from London whose population had
dropped to below seven million for the first time since 1901.

The Underground

There we were in the vaulted tunnel, running:
You in your going-away coat speeding ahead
And me – me, then, like a fleet god gaining
Upon you before you turned to a reed

Or some new white flower slashed with crimson
As the coat flapped wild and button after button
Sprang off and fell in a trail
Between the underground and the Albert Hall.

Honeymooning, moonlighting, late for the Proms,
Our echoes die in the corridor and now
I come as Hansel came on the moonlit stones
Retracing the path back, lifting the buttons

To end up in a draughty lamplit station
After the trains have gone, the wet track
Bared and tensed as I am, all attention
For your step following and damned if I look back.

SEAMUS HEANEY (1981)

154

Maquis

Along the pavement ragwort daisies stand,
sentinels of some primeval land
lying beneath the concrete.
Their round yellow faces stare
from every crevice where
they keep their watch.

Down by Chapel Market there's a bulldozed block
waiting for the builders, enclosed
with corrugated iron.
Through the chinks one sees
sapling trees,
willowherb and briars,
birds, butterflies and bees.

That's after two years. Give it twenty, even ten,
and through the concrete would erupt again
the forest that was London.
Like a nemesis that brings
catastrophe, this maquis clings
through time and waits,
patiently watching in the wings.

SHONA BURNS (1976)

London Pride

London Pride has been handed down to us.
London Pride is a flower that's free.
London Pride means our own dear town to us,
And our pride it for ever will be.
Woa, Liza,
See the coster barrows,
Vegetable marrows
And the fruit piled high.
Woa, Liza,
Little London sparrows,
Covent Garden Market where the costers cry.
Cockney feet
Mark the beat of history.
Every street
Pins a memory down.
Nothing ever can quite replace
The grace of London Town.

There's a little city flower every spring unfailing
Growing in the crevices by some London railing,
Though it has a Latin name, in town and countryside
We in England call it London Pride.

London Pride has been handed down to us.
London Pride is a flower that's free.
London Pride means our own dear town to us,
And our pride it for ever will be.
Hey, lady,
When the day is dawning
See the policeman yawning
On his lonely beat.
Gay lady,
Mayfair in the morning,
Hear your footsteps echo in the empty street.
Early rain
And the pavement's glistening.

All Park Lane
In a shimmering gown.
Nothing ever could break or harm
The charm of London Town.

In our city darkened now, street and square and crescent
We can feel our living past in our shadowed present,
Ghosts beside our starlit Thames
Who lived and loved and died
Keep throughout the ages London Pride.

London Pride has been handed down to us.
London Pride is a flower that's free.
London Pride means our own dear town to us,
And our pride it for ever will be.
Grey city
Stubbornly implanted,
Taken so for granted
For a thousand years.
Stay, city,
Smokily enchanted,
Cradle of our memories and hopes and fears.
Every Blitz
Your resistance
Toughening,
From the Ritz
To the Anchor and Crown,
Nothing ever could override
The pride of London Town.

NOËL COWARD (1941)

157

Acknowledgements

The editor and publishers wish to thank the following poets, poets' executors and estates, publishers and literary agents, who are the copyright holders in each case, for permission to reproduce poems and lyrics and extracts from poems and lyrics as listed below:

The Earl Attlee for a poem by Clement Attlee;
Elizabeth Bartlett for two previously unpublished poems;
John Milne and Peter Porter for a poem by Martin Bell;
Harry Chambers/Peterloo Poets for a poem by Connie Bensley from *Progress Report* (1981);
John Murray (Publishers) Ltd for three poems by John Betjeman from *Collected Poems* (1958);
Nyki Blatchley for a poem from *Stratford Poets Book 2* (published from 10 Tern Gardens, Cranham, Upminster);
Macmillan Publishers Ltd for two poems by Alan Brownjohn from *The Railings* (1961), *Sandgrains On A Tray* (1969) and an extract from a poem from *Warrior's Career* (1972);
Shona Burns for a poem from *Along The Pavement* (Outposts Publications, 1976) and two poems © 1981;
'P.B.' for a poem from *I Want To Write It Down* (Peckham Publishing Project, 1980);
The Estate of the late Richard Church for a poem from *The Collected Poems Of Richard Church* (Dent, 1948);
Chappell Music Ltd for lyrics from three songs by Noël Coward (two of which are quoted in part only in this book), ©1941, 1954 and 1963, words and music by Noël Coward;
Rosemarie Dale for a poem from *Stepney Words I & II* (Centerprise Publications, 136 Kingsland High Street, London E8, 1978);
J. D. Lewis & Sons for a poem by Tom Earley;
Gavin Ewart for two poems from *The Collected Ewart 1933–1980* (Hutchinson);

Harry Chambers/Peterloo Poets for a poem by U. A. Fanthorpe to be published in *Standing To* (1982);

The Estate of Michael Flanders for the lyrics of a song from *The Songs Of Flanders And Swann* (Elm Tree Books and St George's Press, 1977);

Graham Greene for a poem from *Babbling April* (Blackwell); Michael Hamburger for a poem from *Travelling* (Fulcrum Press, 1969) and Carcanet Press for a poem by Michael Hamburger from *Ownerless Earth*;

Milly Harris for a poem from *Stepney Words I & II* (Center-prise Publications, 136 Kingsland High Street, London E8, 1978);

Mark Haviland for a poem originally published by the Tower Hamlets Arts Project, 178 Whitechapel Road, London E1;

Seamus Heaney for a poem from *Thames Poetry Vol II*, *No 9* (published from 160 High Road, Wealdstone, Harrow, Middlesex);

David Higham Associates Ltd for two poems by John Heath-Stubbs from *Selected Poems* (Oxford University Press) and *Satires and Epigrams* (Turret, 1968);

Punch Publications Ltd for a poem by E. V. Knox;

London Magazine Editions for an extract from a poem by Herbert Lomas from *Private And Confidential*, 1974, and Herbert Lomas for previously unpublished poem;

Stormking Music, New York for the lyrics of two songs by Ewan MacColl;

Faber And Faber Ltd for a poem from *The Collected Poems Of Louis MacNeice*;

Michael Joseph Ltd for two poems by Spike Milligan from *Open Heart University*;

Associated Book Publishers Ltd and the Canadian publishers, McClelland and Stewart Ltd, for a poem by A. A. Milne from *When We Were Very Young*;

Jonathan Cape Ltd for a poem from *Out Loud* and two poems from *The Apeman Cometh* by Adrian Mitchell;

Gerald Duckworth & Co Ltd for a poem by Harold Munro from *Collected Poems*;

John Murray (Publishers) Ltd for lines by Alfred Noyes from *The Barrel-Organ*;

Oxford University Press for a poem by Christopher Reid from *The Imperial War Museum* (1979);

Alan Ross for a poem from *Poems 1942-67* (Eyre & Spottiswoode, 1967);

Olga Katzin Miller for a poem by Sagittarius;

Carcanet Press Ltd for two poems by C. H. Sisson from *To The Gods The Shades* and *In The Trojan Ditch*;

Chatto and Windus Ltd for three poems by Jon Stallworthy from *Root And Branch*;

Bernie Steer for a poem © Bernie Steer 1975;

The Director of the Whitechapel Art Gallery for a poem by Avram Stencl first published in the Gallery's Catalogue for Summer 1972;

W. J. Strachan for two poems originally published in *The Seasons Pause* (Secker & Warburg, 1950);

Mr Hubert Nicholson for a poem by A. S. J. Tessimond from *Not Love Perhaps* (Autolycus Publications);

'M.S.' for a poem from *I Want To Write It Down: Writing By Women In Peckham*, 1980, (from Peckham Publishing Project, The Bookplace, 13 Peckham High Street, London SE15);

Christopher Todd for a poem by Ruthven Todd from *The Terrible Rain* (edited by Brian Gardner, Eyre Methuen);

Victor Gollancz Ltd and the Canadian publisher, Random House Inc, for a poem by John Updike from *Hoping For A Hoopoe*; (Gollancz) and *The Carpentered Hen* (Random House);

Vivian Usherwood for a poem from *Poems* (Centerprise Publishing Project, 1975);

A. M. Heath & Co Ltd and Thomas Y. Crowell Co, the Canadian publisher, for a poem by Judith Viorst from *People And Other Aggravations*;

Gaberbocchus Press/Uitgeverij De Harmonie (Amsterdam) for a poem by Eugene Walter from *The Shapes Of The River*;

Michelene Wandor for a previously unpublished poem;

Lady Wilson for a poem from *Selected Poems* (Hutchinson, 1970);

Free Man's Press Editions for a poem by Gerry Wells from *A Backward Look* (1980);

Ms Ann Wolfe for extracts from two poems by Humbert Wolfe from *The Uncelestial City* and *Kensington Gardens* (Gollancz);

Carcanet Press Ltd for two poems by David Wright from *Metrical Observations* and *To The Gods The Shades*; Chatto & Windus Ltd for a poem by Peter Yates from *Light And Dark*.

Every effort has been made to trace copyright holders but, in one or two cases, without success. The editor and publishers wish to apologise for consequent omissions.

The editor wishes to thank Geoffrey Strachan for his advice in the compilation of this anthology and also Christina Dunhill, whose assistance in discovering poems and tracing their sources has been invaluable. One of the great joys for poetry lovers in London is the existence of the Arts Council Poetry Library in Long Acre, which is run by a true friend of poetry, Jonathan Barker: to him, too, thanks are due.

Textual Note: Where the original text of a poem has been abridged, omissions from the original are indicated by three dots following the full stop. Where a title has been given to an extract from a long poem the original title of the poem is given after the poet's name.

Notes

'M.S.': First Impressions
This poem is from an anthology of writing by women in Peckham called *I Want To Write It Down*.

James Thompson: Sunday At Hampstead
James Thompson was a pauper and a drunkard who wrote the most famous atheist poem of the nineteenth century, 'The City Of Dreadful Night'. He used to walk around London on winter nights in frayed bedroom slippers. When he finally collapsed from internal bleeding he was buried in Highgate Cemetery. His poems paid for his coffin.

Michelene Wandor
Michelene Wandor is a poet, critic and playwright for stage, television and radio. Her new poetry collection, *Upbeat*, was published this February by Journeyman Press.

Shona Burns
Shona Burns lives in Hackney. Since reading English at Cambridge she has worked as a typist, freelance editor, cabaret singer and journalist. Her first collection, *Along The Pavement*, was published in 1976.

Elizabeth Bartlett
Elizabeth Bartlett writes of herself 'I was born of working class parents near the Kent coalfields in 1923. My father was an ex-sergeant in the army and my mother a house-parlour-maid. Educated at an elementary school, I won a scholarship to grammar school, only to be removed at the age of 15 to work in a hypodermic needle factory. I started writing poetry at school and was first published at the age of 19. I cannot explain a life-long passion for this private art.' Her first collection, *A Lifetime of Dying*, was published in 1979.

Tom Earley: Post Office Tower
Tom Earley, born in Wales, educated in London, lives now as a writer in Bloomsbury. He describes himself as a libertarian socialist. An active pacifist since 1937, he has now joined Plaid Cymru.

Isaac Rosenberg: Fleet Street
The third stanza quoted on page 60 is an early draft. In the final printed version of the poem it reads as follows:

> The stony buildings blindly stare
> Unconscious of the crime within,
> While man returns his fellow's glare
> The secrets of his soul to win.
> And each man passes from his place,
> None heed. A shadow leaves such trace.

Harold Monro: The Ocean In London
Harold Monro founded the *Poetry Review* in 1912 and then opened the Poetry Bookshop in Devonshire Street and later in Bloomsbury. He ran the Poetry Bookshop until 1936 – the first serious attempt to sell poetry in England. He supported and published many young poets, but alcohol took its toll and when he died hardly any of them went to his funeral.

Avram Stencl: Whitechapel In Britain
Avram Stencl was born in Poland and came to London in 1934. His poem which was translated from the Yiddish was published in the Whitechapel Art Gallery's catalogue for 1972.

Vivian Usherwood: Hackney
Some children join riots; some write it down. This poignant piece of lyrical invective is one of a collection of poems by Vivian Usherwood all written when he was twelve years old.

Rosemarie Dale: Stepney
This poem is one from a collection, *Stepney Words* edited by a schoolteacher, Chris Searle, the publication of which in 1971 resulted in him being dismissed from his job.

U. A. Fanthorpe: Rising Damp
U. A. Fanthorpe was born in Kent in 1929. After graduating from St Anne's Oxford she became a teacher. Now she works as a hospital receptionist in Bristol. Her first collection, *Side Effects* (Harry Chambers/Peterloo Poets), was published in 1978.

Gerry Wells
Gerry Wells served in the war in the same regiment as Keith Douglas and has produced two volumes of poetry, *A Backwards Look* and *Obie's War*, written thirty years after the events they describe.

Connie Bensley: Vauxhall
Connie Bensley lives in South West London where she was born and which she has left only during war-time evacuation. She has worked as a secretary to a medical practice. Her first collection of poetry, *Progress Report*, was published by Harry Chambers/Peterloo Poets in 1981.

'P.B.' High Rise In Peckham
'P.B.' is one of the contributors to an anthology of writing by women in Peckham called *I Want To Write It Down* from which this poem is taken.

Index of Poets

Index Of First Lines

172